WOMEN DATING AND BEING IRRESISTIBLE

*16 Ways to Make Him Crave
and Keep His Attention*

RACHEL ROSE

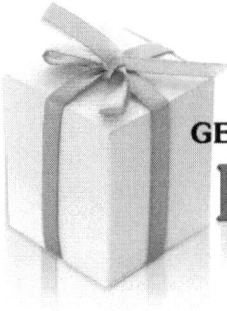

GET YOUR
FREE GIFT!

WAIT! – DO YOU LIKE FREE BOOKS?

My **FREE Gift** to You!! As a way to say **Thank You** for downloading my book, I'd like to offer you more **FREE BOOKS!** Each time we release a NEW book, we offer it first to a small number of people as a test - drive. Because of your commitment here in downloading my book, I'd love for you to be a part of this group. You can join easily here → **http://www. makehimcraveyou.com**

If you're interested in having an *outstandingly passionate relationship* in all areas you **MUST** signup for these **FREE BOOKS!** It's easy to join by going here → **http://www.makehimcraveyou.com**

CONTENTS

INTRODUCTION

Matters of the heart, whether its relationships, affairs, or whatever name you choose to give it, are often tricky. Relationship entails managing each other as well as pesky emotions in the bargain; but we all crave them because that's just the way we are wired.

When it comes to men, women tend to get a bit confused sometimes as to how to get what they want from them. In a world teeming with thousands of beautiful, bold and attractive women, it is not surprising that the first thing most of us want from a man is his attention. It makes perfect sense of course, when you consider that his attention is vital if you are going to get him to so much as look in your direction, never mind talk to you.

Whether you want to snag a man's attention for two hours or twenty years, there are a lot of rules for doing that.

Fortunately, men are like maps which means when you take the steps you should, you often arrive at the destination you want — that may sound corny to you, but I assure you it's true.

A man's attention is a very easy thing to snag and if you aren't doing that, then I am willing to bet you are doing a lot of things wrong as you will see in chapter one of this book.

A man's attention is however a fleeting thing if you do not play your cards right because men are easily bored sometimes which is why this book is divided into three parts. Part three tells you how to keep his attention once you finally have it.

There are rules to relationships and really, with men, it never pays you to break the rules. Now while it's true that men generally do the chasing, you are not going to be able to attract his attention just by existing. You have to take proactive action too. And when you have caught that attention, you are guaranteed to lose it in a heartbeat too if you do not know what you are about.

CHAPTER ONE

What You've Been Doing Wrong

If you are like everyone else, and I am going to take a wild stab and guess that you are, you probably want romance and happy endings with that perfect someone who loves you all to pieces; charms, warts, and all. Now don't worry, that's a completely normal desire, and we're all guilty as charged.

At this point though, I should probably point out that the 'he' in question is not just any random John Doe who crawls into your life off the fire escape. *He* is that special guy who makes your breath hitch a little in your chest, makes you believe in magic, makes you giggle like a child, and makes you tingle in all the good places with a mere glance.

Whether he's someone whose eyes you met across a large ballroom few seconds ago, or he's the friendly co-worker you've been eyeing, or he's the platonic friend you would like to turn into something more, there are sure-fire ways to attract a man for keeps. None of these skills were necessarily natural talents for anyone; they are simple arts which every woman can learn to get men attracted to her. If you've been having trouble attracting men and getting a date, you may be unknowingly sending out vibes that push men away. I'm willing to bet you already know that men have different thought processes from women and given we've established that, you need to understand how the male psyche works in order to get his attention. You need to know what to do to grab his attention.

On some level, everyone craves love, romance and happily-ever-after because it's in our nature as humans to want love, acceptance and companionship. Unfortunately though, despite how much you want to attract his attention, you could simply end up pushing him far away and straight into someone else's arms.

The unwritten rules of relationships state that men have to be attracted before they give chase and while nothing prevents *you* from giving chase if you see a male specimen you like; it's that much more delicious, exciting, and wonderfully sinful to be the object of hot, focused, ardent, passionate pursuit— trust me!

The Victorian ladies had this down to a fine art; setting their sights on a man, and getting *him* to do the chasing. Now while we all know this is the 21st century, the truth remains that testosterone hasn't changed much and it still produces pretty much the same effect in men.

If you have ever wanted a man so badly, it hurt, and yet had to watch him indicate interest in every woman but you then I am willing to bet that you are definitely doing a lot of things wrong. You may not necessarily like all I have to say because they may hit a sore spot or two, but in truth, you'll be better for it so you might want to keep reading.

Whether you already have him and are looking to keep him or you just plain want to attract him in the first place, this book is definitely for you; and yes, there are some things you should watch out for in both scenarios.

Men are complex creatures; incredibly simple and yet incredibly complicated. There are some things you're probably doing that repel rather than attract men. Simple, everyday things your girlfriends would likely applaud because they make sense to a woman and not a man. Well if you are trying to attract your own sex, then there is likely no harm done; but if your aim is to attract and keep a man's attention you might want to avoid doing the following:

1. Being invisible

Some women are naturally shy and have a way of fading into the woodwork in any room. Some others are not a bit shy but they are so wrapped up in school, work or some other projects that they rarely have time to go get a life, never mind a social life. Either way, here's a simple sentence for you: *you have to be seen to be favoured*. You may have the finest attributes of a modern-day Rosa Parks, Florence Nightingale, Mata Hari, and Cleopatra all rolled up into one, but no man is going to break down your door and force his way into your house just to chat you up and find out if you are interesting. You have to get out there!

Come on, when was the last time you placed an order for a custom-made *haute couture* cocktail dress from a designer you had never heard of, residing in a country which even Google map does not know exists? Exactly! You can only want something you have at least heard about or seen. Even your soul mate isn't gonna want you if he doesn't know you exist—literally.

Every woman is a perfect jewel that should be admired and appreciated but until you believe that and learn to sparkle in all your wonderful uniqueness, you will definitely have some lonely days — or years — ahead.

Go out every now and then with a girlfriend or two; and as you've probably heard, men find it harder to approach a woman when she's with a crowd of girlfriends. When you have two friends with you, they can very easily keep each other company if a guy walks up to you, so it's win-win really. Even when you do go out with a crowd of friends, make certain to pick a few minutes to go sit alone at the bar or something. Don't be too obvious about it, but do find a way to split off from the pack a little. It will make it that much easier for a man to work up the courage to approach you.

Not to diss the importance of a platonic male friend, but unless he's so apparently gay that even a blind man couldn't miss it, you might want to minimize the number of times you go out with such male friends if your aim is to attract other guys. Guys tend to be territorial and if he sees you with a guy on a night out, the logical assumption would be that you are an item and he'll most likely keep his distance. Of course this rule does not apply if said platonic male friend invites you out on a date with his other guy friends because hey, one of them just may be Mr Right.

2. Maintaining the same zip code year in, year out.

Now I don't know about you, but I've certainly seen women who spent years trying to get even the most homely, pot-bellied, middle-aged mailman in their locality to say hello with no success; but the first time they took a mere two weeks vacation in a new place, they got as much as four different men interested in them and hot on the pursuit. What changed, you may ask. Well in truth, not much. Sometimes, a precious stone (that would be you) needs a new and different setting (that would be your location) to be better appreciated.

Every now and then, you need to shake the home dust off your sandals and hop on a flight to someplace you've probably never been. Apart from the incredible good having a sense of adventure does to you, it also makes it possible for you to meet new people who could have a positive influence on our personal and professional life. Plus, it's a wonderful de-stressor and even if you don't meet anyone new, I am willing to bet you'd return from your trip that much happier, positive and receptive to new people.

3. Busting his chops, especially when you've just met each other.

Okay everyone loves a woman who knows her own mind and all, but in truth, an alarming number of men happen to have surprisingly fragile egos neatly tucked away beneath all that brawn and delicious masculinity. No, this does not mean you have to navigate through every conversation like it's filled with verbal landmines with the sensitivity of egg shells, but it does mean you need to dial back the screaming-harpy persona a touch.

Be yourself by all means, but try not to regale every stranger you meet with tales of how your ex had the face of a toad and the brains of a jitterbug. In fact, even down the road of a long, happy relationship, try not to diss your ex too much in front of your current love interest. It may seem like solidarity to you, but he wouldn't be human if he didn't privately wonder if this would be his fate if your relationship does not work out. Keep the labels and insults for girls' night outs if you really need to get it off your chest; and even then, only do that with your most trusted BFF.

If a man likes you, what you think matters a great deal to him despite how much he may act otherwise so a little tact and diplomacy is a definite way to go. If you proceed to let him know on say, the first date, how you think he's a wimp for letting his boss ride roughshod over him, you might as well pack up and go home; date night's over.

Guys are humans and prone to making a lot of mistakes; I like to think it's probably as a result of all that testosterone poisoning. But just because you're afraid of busting his chops doesn't mean you have to roll over and play dead every time he steps out of line. Feel free to let him have it; he'll respect you more for it. But at the same time, do not over-react or go overboard with the reprimand coz that would definitely constitute busting his chops and neither one of you wants that.

4. Pretending it doesn't matter to you

No I've not asked you to wear your heart on your sleeve and a paper-bag over your head that says, "Single and desperately searching". But the truth is, we are humans and our makeup is such that we unconsciously give off vibes based on our inner thoughts and convictions. For as long as you pretend that it does not matter to you if not even one man admires you in six months, the more you will continue to subconsciously send the wrong message to guys that keeps them away.

Men love to do the chasing, but knowing you want them to, makes it easier all around. So while you're probably going to issue a feminine growl of dissent at the next sentence, the truth is that knowing you are a hot, attractive, gorgeous woman in her prime who has men tripping all over their own feet to say hello, does wonders for your self-esteem. Studies have shown for instance that women who have suffered one form of abuse or the other went on to blossom under the sincere appreciation and love of another man. It's really just a fact of nature that little can change; being chased is good for you, being in love and having it reciprocated is also good for you. Pretending you don't mind that you're not being chased is a very poor form of playing hard to get that just leaves you lonely with your emotions in tatters.

5.   Pretending you don't need anyone

Now unless you were a conjoined twin at birth, you most probably came into this world on your own; I mean even regular twins don't come into the world together, just one after the other. But the truth is, when it comes down to it, no one is an island. Everyone needs human contact every now and then; even the most veritable recluse.

For some of us, being strong, independent women is very important and we strive so hard to achieve this persona that we often get it and more. These days, there are a lot of strong, independent — and lonely — women around. These women are often endowed with some of the most beautiful characteristics you could hope to find in any human being but they often end up alone and sad.

No this is not the part where I tell you men have fragile egos that need to be kowtowed to; this is the part where I remind you that everyone loves to be needed.

6.   You make the first move

Yes I know this is the twenty-first century and playing hard to get probably sounds like something straight out of a forties movie to you. However, in truth, the worst thing you can do is to smother a guy with too much... you! As sweet as it may seem on paper to tattoo his name onto your ass and start showing up at his apartment every morning with breakfast after date two, you'll just come across as desperate. Men are attracted to the thrill of the chase, so if you're chasing after him, you're inadvertently taking away the challenge and forcing him into the role of the hunted. Keep it low-key and keep him on the edge of his seat whilst maintaining your composure. Frankly, being chased is a pretty good feeling so you need to learn to sit back like the jewel you are, and just sparkle. Let *him* run himself ragged chasing after you; he will value that much more in the end.

7.   You talk dirty

Unless you are a trucker who was raised by wolves, you really have no business talking dirty as a lady. It may seem like another basis for gender equality but swearing and cussing doesn't sit too good especially when it's coming from your perfect lips. When you have just met a man, you should really try to keep the swear words to a minimum as polls have shown that it can be a huge turn-off. Come on, men aren't alone in this. Remember the last time you shot that colleague at the office a dirty look accompanied by a chiding, "Language, please." Yeah dirty talk, especially in people you don't know very well, gives the impression that they don't have good manners.

Some of us love to bitch; we don't mean any harm though, it's just how we blow off steam. We bitch about everyone from our boss, to our co-workers, to our friends, to that greasy-haired man who cut us off in traffic, and we sometimes even bitch about the waiter and the poor service. It's human nature to complain, but that doesn't mean it's right. If you know your Bible stories, you probably remember how snakes were used to punish the Israelites for complaining huh? As much as possible, try to avoid bitching when you are trying to get a man interested in you because men are really straight forward. If he thinks you are a bitch, he may write you off before he's even had a chance to get to know you. Talk about starting off on the wrong foot!

8. You try too hard

Okay this one is so classic, it's practically vintage. Men tend to get bored easily; in fact more male children are prone to ADHD; don't ask me why.

When a man's attention is actually on you, it would likely not stay forever but would shift eventually. And unfortunately this part is where women make mammoth mistakes in trying to make things better.

You start trying too hard to please him and keep his attention on you and in the process, you devalue yourself, put up with insensitive behaviour from him and agree to things that stick in your craw, effectively making yourself into a living, breathing doormat he can walk all over. And he *will* walk all over you because you have in effect taught him to devalue you and when it comes to this one, men are a quick study. There are things he would do to you he wouldn't dare with another woman just because he knows that with you, he can get away with it.

So even though the goal here is to teach you to grab his attention, it is in no way a license for you to chase after him. Let him come to you; let him work for your attention. Yes it sounds like a reversal since *you* want his attention but just go with me on this. Even if you want him to want you, don't make it obvious; do not wear your heart on your sleeve.

These are just some of the ways you've been going about this whole attracting and dating thing the wrong way and if you're honest, you'll admit that you have been guilty of at least one of the above and are next to clueless about how to catch and keep a man's attention. If so, not to worry because here comes the cavalry!

PART TWO – HOW TO CATCH HIS ATTENTION

This part shows you how to catch this

attention for the first time.

CHAPTER TWO

How to Catch His Attention

H ave you ever seen a car salesman trying to convince someone to buy a rickety car with a blown gasket and a bad paint job which looks like it battled with life and lost? Well as incredible as it sounds, that car *will* sell; it just depends on what the salesman thinks of it.

If the salesman honestly believes the car is a good product and would really like to drive it himself, that car would sell so fast it would probably leave a trail of heart-broken would-be buyers behind when it did. But if he is just trying to con some unsuspecting poor sod into buying a car he wouldn't be caught dead in, he could try unsuccessfully for years. The irony of it is, the salesman who honestly likes the car on his hands, will likely sell a very old car faster than a salesman who detests the fairly used, relatively sound car he is trying to pawn off.

Forget car analogies; you can't get people interested in you if you aren't interested in you. Have you ever heard the expression; "You train people on how to treat you". It may be the oldest cliché in the book but it remains as true now as it was the first time it was ever said.

Just in case you weren't listening the first time around here's a repeat; *you will never convince anyone that you matter until you honestly believe it yourself!*

You have to catch your own attention before you can hope to catch someone else's. No matter what else is going on around you, you have to genuinely love yourself and appreciate yourself before you can hope to get someone else to do the same. Most times, people forget that they need to love themselves and this is always a recipe for disaster. No one ever enjoyed a relationship with an insecure, unhappy person; in fact most people run in the other direction if they find they are in the presence of just such a person because negativity rubs off very easily and no one wants extra baggage.

Flitting through life, and sparing no thoughts for your inner self is sadly easy to do, but the overall effects of just such an existence are subtle and yet dangerous. For most of us, we are our own worst critic. Come on, you know exactly what I'm talking about. Remember when you wore that new jacket to the office and while all your co-workers couldn't stop cooing, you privately thought you looked fat in it? Exactly!

People learn to put themselves down more easily than they learn to praise themselves. Unfortunately, self-esteem and confidence are kinda hard to come by when you have a hard time viewing yourself in a good light.

Luckily, that can be changed if you are willing to try a few of these steps:

1. Decide on who exactly you want to be

Okay I can almost hear you wondering why you need to go on a philosophical trip of self-discovery when all you want is just to catch the attention of the friendly guy next-door. Never underestimate the power of body language though; and while guys may not get women most times, they often instinctively smell desperation from a mile away. There is a little desperation that comes from not knowing exactly who you are or where you fit in the scheme of things. A little self-evaluation never hurt anyone you know?

If your aim is to catch the attention of the perfect man for you, the first thing you want to do is examine yourself. Would you date someone like yourself if you could? Do you have the temperament of a fishwife or of a regular all-American girl?

Examine yourself as objectively as possible and then decide on who exactly you want to be before you start working towards that. For the record, you should decide to be the best version of yourself; work on your weaknesses and magnify your strengths.

When you know exactly who you are, you tend to be comfortable in your own skin and let me tell you, few things are as powerful when it comes to attracting the opposite sex. A girl who knows who she is and what she wants out of life will often come across as bold, confident, and supremely able to hold her own anywhere. Men will often admire and respect such a person and frankly, with the kind of vibes such sexy confidence gives off, she may well need to stave guys off with a stick!

2. Forgive yourself for your past mistakes

You know the way it's easier to forgive a stranger for cutting you off in line at the check-out point than it is to forgive your BFF for forgetting you hated anchovies on your pizza? Sometimes it really *is* easier to forgive everyone but yourself.

Now don't get me wrong, I applaud an amazing sense of responsibility and the ability to feel guilt for mistakes but you have to take stock and move on. Don't remain stuck in the past because the mistakes you don't forgive yourself for, you will likely repeat.

Whether it's baggage from past relationships, career problems or whatever, you need to throw down the weight as much as possible. The longer you carry it around, the more you'll edge into bitterness without even realising it and that's certainly not how you want the man of your dreams to meet you is it?

3.   Do the things that make you happy

Yes this is the part where I tell you that unless you follow your dreams, you will lead a life of quiet — or noisy, depending on your personality — desperation. Come on everyone has that one thing that never fails to lift them from the slumps every time they do it. It could be everything from singing, to writing, to playing with the stock market. Whatever it is that gets your blood flowing that much faster, do it as often as you can without apologies as that is the one thing guaranteed to make you glow with happiness from the inside out.

Whatever it is that makes you feel good about yourself, do it because the more you do, the more fulfilled you will be and yes, the more attractive you'll be.

Most single women make the mistake of living their lives like they are waiting to exhale. You know Sleeping Beauty was a great cartoon but in truth, you don't want to spend your life waiting to be kissed by a Prince before you start living. Keep busy and have fun every step of the way; and that's how you attract the right people into your life — and yes, that applies to both sexes.

4.   Don't take yourself too seriously

Laughter is such a powerful and yet often overlooked aphrodisiac. I can't tell you how many men fell for their wives when they first met because they were attracted by her sense of humour. Life is a drag for most people whether they admit it or not and everyone wants people in their lives who help them let go of the stress and have fun. Having a sense of humour means you know how to have fun and men are often attracted to fun-loving girls. So if you want to attract love sometime in the future, learn to laugh a lot in the present.

Apart from the fact that you want to attract his attention, you want to be alive and healthy long enough to enjoy it right? Laughter protects you against heart attack by improving functions of blood vessels and increasing blood flow.

A good hearty laughter releases stress and tension and relaxes the whole body for up to a good 45 minutes. Of course it also triggers a release of feel-good hormones and gives you that extra sparkle that makes you infinitely more attractive to someone like the guy you've been checking out.

Being fun, outgoing, pleasant, happy and positive may sound like an uphill task if you usually have the temperament of a regular Scrooge but let's face it, being lacking in what the French call joie de vivre (zest for life) has caused you more harm than good and you know it!

Happiness really is a decision. No matter what else is going on in your life, you can be happy if you decide to be. On the flip side, no matter how good you have got it, you can be the most unhappy and miserable person that ever lived if you choose. Find things that get your blood rushing through your veins and do it! If that job is sucking all the joy and laughter out of you, then quit and do something that makes you fulfilled no matter how risky it may seem.

There is a lot to be said for living on the edge; people who take risks tend to live longer and better than people who play it safe.

A girl who knows how to laugh will light any room up the moment she walks into it and yes, the gentlemen will be lining up in droves! What do you think made Serena Van Der Woodsen such a hit with the guys on the Upper East Side? Humour, wit, charm and sexy confidence will do all your talking for you before you even open your mouth!

5.   Learn to love your own company

Being self-sufficient is a definite goal for some people, and no wonder when you consider that it is far easier to loathe being alone than to learn to enjoy being by yourself. Before you can learn to attract attention, you have to learn love your own company otherwise it would be a hard sell. Being alone actually brings a certain freedom with it that few people stop to appreciate and when you can enjoy your own company, you will find that you are less desperate for the company of others. Life is nothing but ironies of course; a healthy social life begins with learning to be comfortable being by yourself. Attracting attention begins with attracting your own attention; take it or leave it, humans have a sixth sense for this sort of things. Quiet desperation drives other people far, far, way whilst confident self-assurance makes them want to spend all day with you.

Fear of your own company is actually a dreadful fate because it forces you to accept social situations or companions you would ordinarily not be comfortable with.

If you can sincerely say that you are alright being alone or in mixed company with other people, then you should count yourself blessed because you have managed to strike that delicate balance that many people try to find but which only few are able to achieve.

Self-respect and a good sense of self-worth are more important than most people realize in a relationship and it's often best to know where you stand in your own estimation before you get into a relationship with another human being. Studies have shown that women who sincerely love and appreciate themselves end up with men who do the same. Whereas women who think ill of themselves often end up being doormats in relationships; you have to learn to stand up for yourself or else, down the line, no one will.

Men dig girls they can respect. If he doesn't respect you, he may still be attracted to you, after all men are visual. But in that case, once he gets to hit the sheets with you, he loses interest very quickly and if you're reading this book, I'm assuming you don't want that now, do you?

CHAPTER THREE

Use the Goods

O kay, get your mind out of the gutter; I haven't asked you to use your body as bait to get what you want! There are several weapons in your arsenal which you are probably not using to your advantage now, none of which is necessarily your body. At the risk of sounding like a broken record, men *are* visual; so learn to maximize your attraction by showing off your physical attributes in the best light possible.

Nature definitely had in mind the fact that men are visual when she endowed women with a lot of fine, eye-catching qualities but unfortunately, some women deliberately or inadvertently, choose to ignore these powerful gifts they possess rather than utilizing them to reach their maximum potential.

Using what you have simply entails making certain you show off your best qualities without over-playing your hand; I mean you get bonus points if your efforts seem... well, effortless.

It never hurts you to be great eye candy and the best part is, if the guy you are tripping for does not notice, you may be likely to attract the attention of some other hunk and well know how much guys love rivalry. So here are a few tips you could try to make sure you stand out in a crowd:

1.   Groom yourself

Women are naturally endowed with hormones and features which make them vastly different from, and infinitely more attractive to men. Most women make the mistake of buying into the 'beauty is on the inside' mantra and let themselves go on the outside. Don't get me wrong, beauty *is* on the inside but that's no call for you to turn up for your first date with your hair like a bird's nest and your armpits stinking to high heavens!

Come on, you probably know a person or two who have emotional issues the size of the Great Canyon because they let themselves go on the outside. Looking good is good business and not just for him, but for you. There is a confidence that comes from knowing you look your absolute best. It's the kind of confidence that can have you walk into a room like you own the place; and let me tell you, you can't put a price tag on that kind of confidence. It draws men *and* women to you like flies! Suddenly you are the centre of attention; every woman wants to be you and every man wants to date you. If that isn't a dream come true, I don't know what is.

When it comes to looking good, the devil is in the details. Get a flattering hairstyle and go ahead and book that spa weekend you have been dying to get. Get a massage, get a facial, and treat yourself to the very best because life you have right now isn't a rehearsal; it's the real deal.

Your body is a model of perfection; regardless of whether you have Eva Longoria's body or not and you have to treat it as such. At this point, I'm willing to bet you've heard that men are attracted first and foremost by what they see. Come on, do a simple poll of say, five of all your male friends; I'm willing to bet 5 out of 5 do an immediate scope of every woman in a yard radius once they walk into a room.

Men are visual, and while you may have heard that *ad nauseum*, it *is* true. It's just the way guys are wired. You *should* have a great personality yes, but your appearance is really usually the first, second, and maybe third thing a guy will notice when he meets you first. That may sound shallow and all, but it's true; men notice your drab appearance first before they notice your sparkling personality and in the world of dating, first impression matters a hell of a lot. I mean, when was the last time you heard a guy say, "Hey check out the personality on that girl." Exactly!

Groom yourself, pamper yourself and flatter your features because when it comes down to it, a man's sexual organs are more in his eyes than in his pants.

2.   Drape yourself in the very best for you

This is the part where I encourage you to dress to kill! Your wardrobe says more about you than you realize and the first rule of thumb when it comes to picking out clothes is to never assume that there is a 'one style fits all' cloth in existence. We all have different body shapes, sizes and so on, thanks to the Great Artist; and while slinky, revealing evening gowns may look dazzling on your best friend's rail-thin body, they may not be very flattering on your more voluptuous and rounder curves. So yes, you need to know exactly what type of body figure you have and dress in clothes that flatter you and make you look chic and attractive.

Now don't get me wrong, being dressed to kill does not necessarily mean your clothes ALWAYS have to be in the first stare of fashion. Let's face it, in this economy, you would probably go from plodding along financially to flat broke in a nanosecond if you kept breaking your piggybank to buy Vera Wang's. But do invest in quality clothing; quality over quantity is definitely the way to go. Sometimes it is better to have just five gowns that can go to prom, church, or even the Grammys than to have fifty gowns that cannot go anywhere besides the supermarkets.

Taking care of your body and your appearance are so important, they are virtually the first rule of thumb in attracting a man's attention. It's a principle that never fades: a woman who takes care of herself will attract men easier than one who doesn't. Dress in clothes that make you feel sexy and confident and you can bet you'll exude so much sexy self-assurance that you'll be attracting guys like flies without ever saying a word.

3.   Flatter your body type

If you're like most women you probably think hour-glass is the best body shape to have; well in that case, you would be wrong. In my humble opinion, there is no such thing as a perfect or best body shape. Every figure is amazing, you just have to know what works best and what doesn't; you are in charge of playing up your strengths and flattering your body and appearance with a few tricks as old as femininity. For instance, if you tend to gain weight around the middle (that's the circle shape), you want to avoid clothes that draw attention to that part of your body like high-rise pants and instead go for clothes that fit loosely around the mid-section. If you have what some call the hour-glass shape, you want to avoid tunics, and boxy clothes and go instead for close-fitting and slinky gowns.

Some people's body structures look better in gowns, others are flattered by jeans or skits. It does not matter what you wear, it will not look very good if it is not something that flatters your body type.

4. Go for understated elegance not tawdry exposure

Whatever your body type, try as much as possible to keep it classy by dressing cute, modest and in a way that leaves something to the imagination. Baring it all will only attract the wrong kind of attention. I mean, so long as you're not turning tricks, you don't want men drooling saliva down your chest front do you? There is something classy and insanely sexy about a woman dressed in a style that accentuates her 'assets' whilst hiding skin. Seeing the hint or promise of something underneath and thinking about unveiling what is wrapped up in layers of feminine clothing is what drives men insane with lust. Don't believe me? Ask you male friends.

Men will generally stare at a scantily clad woman but in the end, few decent men would voluntarily approach her. I once took it upon myself to do a small survey involving a hundred men of different races, cultural backgrounds, professions and levels of education. The survey merely involved showing the men two pictures of two women; one was clad in a blue, cocktail gown that stopped somewhere just above her knees and flattered her eyes whilst the other was dressed in a transparent, floor-length gown made completely out of lace with nothing else underneath. The lacy confection was all in black, and sewn to a regal floor-length even though it was completely exposing. Well 95 out of the 100 men said they would rather date the girl in the blue cocktail gown because all her 'goods were not on display'. Got me!

I think the underlying lesson is, tacky is not sexy! Flatter, expose if you must, but don't over play your hand.

5.   Don't be afraid to try colours

Speaking of sexy, bright colours have been known to attract men for as long as humanity can remember. Why else do you think femme fatales from history have been known to favour red, fuschia pink, and such other bold colours? These women frequently brought powerful men to their knees simply by revelling in, and celebrating their own femininity. Lisa Kleen[1] says for the first two years of her job at the District Attorney's office she always wore strictly dark coloured clothes because of her job as an attorney. For the whole of those two years, she rarely got a compliment. One day, she got fed up with the 'dark gloomy colours' and wore a simple red sheath gown to work. She got so many compliments she was walking on air, and at the end of the day, male colleagues who had not so much as noticed her in two years were suddenly asking for her home telephone numbers.

There is something about red that sends an instant erogenous response to the part of the brain that controls passions. It triggers a basic, primal response because it signals sexuality and fertility and makes the opposite sex eager to know you because it's a bold look that few can pull off.

---

1   Not her real name

6.   Observe the rules of makeup and hygiene

Next to diamonds, makeup is a girl's best friend. They could define your features, make you look more alive and awake and even enhance your beauty. But one rule remains true when it comes to makeup; less is more. Before you go out, be sure to apply your makeup as flawlessly as possible; he may not notice, but you will (and so will your confidence) and when it comes down to it, makeup really is for you isn't it?

Colour your puckers too while you're at it. There is just something about a woman in red lipstick that makes her even more visible and attractive to men. Just about every seductress in history has been known to have a signature red lipstick preference. It seems to have a positive effect on men's first impression of your attractiveness. When it comes to makeup though, the rule of thumb remains, less is more. Keep your makeup flawless and as close to natural as possible. Too much could just come off looking trashy.

Good personal hygiene is also a big part of your physical attraction. It helps you immensely if you can smell great and you can do this by showering with bath products with intensely feminine and sensual scents. You should also learn to use a feminine scented deodorant. Most women just try out different perfumes over the years to see what works best, but once you do find one that suits your personality and lifestyle, it would probably be a good idea to make it your signature scent as he will come to associate that particular scent with you. Of course, you know to stay away from the intensely sweet, cloying, sickening fragrance some women favour. It may seem sweet to you, but just irritating and teeth-jarringly sweet to others and frankly for some men, it could be a huge turn-off. It's fine to smell sweet and girly, but just don't go overboard with it, is all because subtlety is key when it comes to body fragrances.

Hygiene does not just end with great scents you know. Yeah, we're thinking your teeth also requires a good brushing every morning and night. Come on, you don't want him running for the hills when you flash him your own version of a come-hither smile, now do you? And while we're on the subject, no you can't get away with bathing once a week, not even if you live in Iceland or somewhere colder; so do try to hop in the shower at least once a day. Frankly, your skin will thank you for it; and if he does approach you, so will his nostrils!

7.   Wear naughty lingerie

No you don't have to strut around in nothing but your under-things, but wearing sexy, naughty, bad, deliciously sinful lingerie beneath your clothes will give you a high like little else and put an unmistakeable spring in your step.

Every time you remember the sexy little number you have on underneath your clothes, you won't be able to stop a secret little smile from crossing your lips. Despite how strait-laced and unimaginative your work clothes may be—yeah surgical scrubs, I'm looking at you— you can still feel like the sexiest most exciting female alive if you have on naughty lingerie beneath your scrubs.

The effect is often that every guy you meet would probably be able to guess from the secret smile playing about your lips that you know something no one else does, and that alone would make him want to come over and satisfy his curiosity as to what you are thinking. A secretive smile lends you an air of mystery and we all know how guys are suckers for adventures.

8.   Be mysterious and unpredictable

No don't scoff; your air of mystery is part of your ladylike charm, just in case you did not know this. A huge part of attracting men is letting them figure you out. Don't talk his ear off, yapping on about every tiny little detail of your life or your feelings. Feel free to hold some things back in a conversation rather than revealing everything with with idle gabbing.

The fact that you can even hold some things back makes you appear more confident than you may be and that air of mystery does wonders for your appeal.

Part of being mysterious is learning not to make yourself available all the time. Every now and then, let him to wonder where you are, what you're doing and who you might possibly be doing it with.

Unpredictability makes you incredibly attractive because as long as he cannot predict what you will do or what you are up to, he will keep watching you in fascination.

9.   Work out

Yes I know it's like a trip to the dentist for some of us, but exercise never goes out of style for several reasons. Hey, working out could even be a good way to meet him and strike up a conversation with him. I mean if say he runs, and you live in the same neighbourhood, what's to stop you from suggesting you run together?

Working out means you remain sculpted, and well-defined in the best way possible which means you end up appearing more attractive and desirable.

Working up a sweat also means that you get to feel good about yourself. There is just something about exercise that triggers your feel good hormones, helps you with anger management and brings out a lot of your awesome qualities.

Exercise makes the blood flow better through your entire body which carries the oxygen and nutrient straight to your skin; a healthy glow is one of the most attractive things ever.

10. Revel in your femininity

Now unless he's gay, every man wants a woman who is so obviously different from him and I think it's just sad when women try so hard to tone down their femininity in the mistaken belief that it is a big turn off for guys. Men and women are created differently with different body types. Usually, where his body is firm and strong, yours is supple and soft. It's the very contrast that sparks an attraction between the sexes.

Learn to play up your differences by dressing in feminine clothes, using feminine perfume, and definitely using heels. High heels are sexy for a variety of reasons; they accentuate your legs and make them appear longer, they make you look more sophisticated, and let's not forget the extra height advantage. High heels also do crazy things to your walk and while you may not appreciate that, he does; trust me!

And while we are putting it out there, you should know that it's not your imagination; you *are* more attractive during your ovulation. Apparently your hormones are more powerful than you realize. It's the same reason most room-mates would swear their cycles synchronize. When you are on your ovulation, your body gives off a vibe that speaks to the animalistic part of humans (or in this case, men); nature's ways of saying you are ready to mate.

Take advantage of the natural sexy hue your body enjoys during this period and go on out for a night out on the town with a girl-friend or two.

Men love coy, feminine gestures, probably for the same reason women love macho, chivalrous men. Fluff your hair every now and then and lean to the side often to give him an unrestricted view of your neck. Guys find this to be cute and attractive as hell.

Be thankful for the body you do have and put your best foot forward!

CHAPTER FOUR

Body Language is Eveything

Body language is the most powerful and effective tool of flirting and while it's not often taught in school, just about everyone can decode the most basic signals. When it comes to the opposite sex, positive body language helps you cinch his interest faster than any words you could speak. In fact, studies have shown that it doesn't matter how pretty or otherwise you are, the most important thing are the signals you send out.

1.   Smile

Imaging you're sitting at a bar and you want that sexy, dimpled guy across the room who's been stealing glances at you to abandon his circle of guy friends and walk up to you, what do you do? It's not rocket science, you smile!

Most of us underestimate the power of a simple smile, little realising it may be the most powerful weapon in the seduction arsenal. Few men will get the courage to approach you when your face looks frowny enough to pulverize rock. And even when they do approach you, they probably wouldn't stick around for long if you keep up the angry-looking expression. A smile softens the lines of your face and makes you look friendly, pleasant, and approachable.

Learn to smile with interest at him, if his attention is what you're after and do it confidently. Most girls do this in a coquettish fashion; you know the head tilted to one side while you treat him to batting lashes and a co-ed smile. It's not necessarily bad, but unless you're sixteen and staring at each other from across the cafeteria at school, that may not be the best way forward. I mean a smile is a smile right and its intention cannot possibly be misunderstood but men are not dummies. If you do the excessive lashes-fluttering thing, he may wonder if you're just toying with him.

In this 21st century, women are going toe-to-toe with men on just about everything; we are in boardrooms, malls, offices, construction sites, you name it. So more often than not, men lack the almost-Neanderthal confidence of the men of old and you need to give them a little helping hand sometimes. A warm, sweet smile tells a guy you would welcome his advances and encourages him to come on over, and keep talking. It does not however mean you have to make it easy for him just because you smiled your encouragement at him; you can totally go ahead and play hard to get when he comes over. (We'll talk more on that below).

Charles Schwab once said that his smile was worth a million dollars; well considering his extraordinary success and penchant for making people fall for him, I do believe he may have understated the truth a little. You can't really put a price tag on the value of your smile because the more you smile the more you enrich your life with new acquaintances and even wonderful love prospects.

A smile is so powerful that even when you speak to your friends or whoever on phone, you can tell when they smile even though you can't see them because it often comes through in their voice and washes over you with its warmth despite how many miles away you are.

Now some of us are a bit shy and would probably melt into a tiny puddle before we would be able to attract the attention of that guy we like; or so we think. Well if that's the case, then you are in luck because I never met a smile that required words. It speaks more eloquently than anything you could say. Think of it as a picture of what's in your mind; it *is* worth a thousand words.

A smile is a necessary part of your accessory. You could be dressed in the height of fashion but until you turn your frown upside down, you won't get much in the way of attention from people. Little Orphan Annie's infamous words, "You are never fully dressed without a smile," should give you a clue. Your smile tells the world that you are someone they would want to get to know.

So the next time you want to catch the attention of everyone from that sexy executive to the cute lifeguard at your favourite holiday beach; catch his gaze and smile! He can't possibly mistake the meaning of that one. And if he doesn't clue in on the first smile, throw a few more his way; it won't hurt.

The ancient Chinese put it best; "A man without a smiling face must not open a shop"

2.   Make eye contact — a lot!

Whoever said 'the eyes are the window to the soul,' certainly knew what they were talking about. Eyes speak so loudly you could probably hear them from across a large ballroom. Come on when was the last time you were unable to correctly decode an angry glare or an admiring gaze? Exactly!

If you are interested in a guy, let him know it by letting your eyes meet his every now and then. Bonus points if you couple it with a smile and if you do this to a guy who is just trying to figure out how to get the courage to walk up to you. Even in a crowded room surrounded by faceless strangers and familiar friends, two people could get lost revelling in each other's gazes.

No you can't just throw him a nervous glance and look away before he even has a chance to meet your gaze. If your aim is to catch a man's attention, you want to let your gaze linger; but not long enough that it becomes creepy though. Just 3-5 seconds of locking eyes with his peepers should do the trick. That length of time would let him know you are definitely interested in him and give him the encouragement to step forward.

If he does approach you, keep up the eye contact as much as you can without going overboard. Apart from making you appear confident, it also creates a sense of intimacy around both of you and gets him even more wrapped up in the conversation.

Eye contact makes a person seem more approachable and the fact remains that people who stand in a corner of a room, arms crossed and eyes down often tend to look less approachable than others.

3.   Lean in towards him

Whenever you're in a conversation with a guy, lean towards him and make him see that you are interested in whatever he's saying. We all have that one friend we feel is an incredible listener so watch what they do for tips. Do they lean back in their chair or cross their arms or face their upper torso away from you in the middle of a conversation? I'm thinking they don't!

Well in that case, borrow a leaf from their book and learn to lean forward a little when listening to a guy. Of course if you overdo it and topple right out of your seat, you're on your own.

Body language is a fine art, subtle without revealing your hand overly-much. We are intelligent humans and by our very make-up, we speak to each other on some other level. Let your body do the talking for you every now and then and learn to flirt subtly with body language. Lean in close to him when you talk and every now and then, touch his hand or shoulder during conversation. You should also learn to turn your body toward him when you two are in close proximity especially your upper torso. Your feet for that matter should also be pointing towards him because body language experts have suggested that when in a conversation; people's feet generally tend to point in a direction they want to go. Crossing your arms is like unconsciously distancing yourself from the conversation or from the person with whom you are conversing. Of course, people generally lean back when they don't like what they hear so you might want to avoid that too, unless of course he just propositioned you within ten minutes of meeting you for the first time.

4.   Watch your posture

Mama was right, no slouching! Whether you are seated at a dinner table, or at your desk at the office or even on the bleachers watching a neighbourhood game, you want to sit straight. Hunching your shoulders makes you appear either afraid to face the world, scared of your own shadow or just furtive, like you've got something nasty to hide; I'm guessing none of those appeal to you huh?

Stick out your chest and straighten your spine. Apart from making you look even more attractive, that posture sticks out your butt *and* your breasts in a good way. If you're conservative, it may sound like just the sort of risqué behaviour Grandmama warned you about; but if you're tired of sitting on the sidelines while other girls get all the good guys, you might want to consider this.

A 1997 study found that the most attractive features in a person fell under changeable aspects of their personality like clothes, hair, *posture*, and weight. Apparently when it comes to dating, most people do not hold onto stuff like your height because that's something over which you really have no control. But something like your posture is something you *can* control and when a guy sees that you put some effort into taking care of your own posture or other such things, it increases your attraction. Dr Jeremy Nicholson of *Psychology Today* is of the view that good posture is sexy, and no wonder because it speaks to health and fitness. No one is attracted to unhealthy looks you know, sad but true.

So the next time you catch yourself slouching or standing wrong, make certain to straighten your shoulders. Good posture facilitates breathing, just in case you didn't know that. Of course the mere fact that you can breathe better thanks to your posture, also means you get more oxygen to your brain thus increasing your ability to think and concentrate. Why else do you think you always found it easier to read that boring philosophy text in college when you were sitting at your desk than when you were curled up on your couch in the foetal position?

Attaining a good posture is a possibility even if you don't have one already. All you have to do is practice constantly until it becomes a part of you. Learn to straighten your shoulders, push out your chest a little and tuck in your stomach. If you can do this and glide across a room with a book perfectly balanced on your head, then you have a good posture.

Getting a good posture takes conscious effort; you have to unlearn the bad habits of the past. A good trick would be to remind yourself constantly by wearing either a wristband or other jewellery that you could see all the time so that every time you clap eyes on it, you will automatically straighten your spine.

5.   Affect a bit of indifference

Show interest, but at the same time make certain you affect a certain nonchalance. Desperation is an accessory no girl should be caught dead in and men can frequently smell it from a mile away. Avoid sending signals that make you seem like you are going to be incomplete without a man in your life. Trust me whether you met four minutes ago or four years ago, desperation remains a definite deal-breaker.

A 'take it or leave it' attitude means you have an easy wrap of confidence around your shoulders and that in itself is guaranteed to perk up his interest. There is just something about guys and challenges; they have a hard time resisting them. If you have an air of indifference rather than a worshipful attitude, you become firmly classified as a challenge in his mind. In which case, put on your running shoes girlfriend because the chase is on!

You should be aware though that some men may be too lazy to chase after you if you seem indifferent, but in my book, that's not necessarily a bad thing. Often, men who can't be bothered to put a little effort into winning a woman are usually only looking for a quick roll in the hay. If this is what you are after yourself, then there's no harm done; but if you envision more than a wham-bam-thank-you-maám, then you might want to run for the hills.

Besides, if you are already not worth the trouble to him, then it's good you see that upfront before you give your heart away to a jerk who is only going to try to make you do the chasing down the road of your relationship. If that does not sound alarm bells in your head, then perhaps you should know that nature never intended women to have to do the chasing in a relationship. If you are a twenty-first century woman, you may scoff at that but in truth, running after a man can be pretty exhausting in the long run; how do you think insecure women are created? You may have him, but you will never really be certain if loves because you put yourself in an uncertain position. When a man has to work to get you and your attention, he tends to appreciate you more; it sounds archaic yes, but trust me it is true.

6.   Touch him

No don't reach for the front of his zipper or his shirt-front; just pat his arm every now and then as you converse. Casual touches between friends are platonic enough and do not overstep any boundaries. Studies have shown that touch increases a connection between parties and both parties are more inclines to show interest and even flirt when they receive casual platonic touches. It isn't one of the five senses for nothing. Humans have been known to die off because they were isolated from other humans and never experienced touch for years.

Even the most casual brush of your hand against his shirt sleeve is an amazing idea. I would usually suggest that you keep it casual because overdoing it could just make you seem too forward and you don't want that; not at this stage. Humans naturally react to touch with warmth and happiness and touching him casually when you are with other people will leave a warm glow in the pit of his stomach.

CHAPTER FIVE

Give then Take - Attention

No one is ever really interested in someone who isn't interested in them. Showing genuine interest in others is how you get them interested in you; it's how you make friends.

Men are as human as the rest of us — shocking, I know, but true. If you are sincerely interested in him, he'll know and he will reciprocate. I'm not saying make the first move mind, I'm just saying don't overdo it with the indifference bit.

Ask questions about him and his life and interest. At this point, you should probably know that some guys, especially the really successful ones, think it's a buzz kill when you start out by asking what they do for a living. More often than not, they mistake the shine in your eyes for dollar signs and that's not a good one is it?

When a guy is attracted to you, he will do little things to impress you like pulling out your chair, holding open car doors, or just plain taking care of his appearance for your date. However little his effort, appreciate it by commenting gently on it; works every single time.

Some ladies take showing interest a step further in a way that really seems to work for them. For instance, you could learn to like some things he does like. No I am in no way suggesting you shove something down your metaphorical throat just to please anyone; hey that would just make you a doormat, and you don't want that. Most guys love football, baseball and so many other sports. Some others just love video games; whatever it is, you could try out a few to see if you like them. In truth, it would most likely be fun and you would learn a few new things. The best part is, even if the evening ends with you deciding you really, really hate football, the most important thing was you tried it because you knew he liked it. He would feel special and much more affectionate towards you.

A friend once told me she cinched her husband's interest when she suggested on date two that they go see a game rather than going to the fancy restaurant he thought she wanted. The night changed from what would have been a stiff, quiet, dignified affair into a memorable evening filled with laughter, teasing, friendly competition and bowling. She didn't know it then, but that was the night he fell in love with her. That was the night he decided she was a keeper.

If this still does not make much sense to you, then picture this; say you had two dates, two nights in a row. Imagine one of those two men spent the first few minutes after he walked in the door playing with your cat (we will call her Sissy) whilst the other sat stiffly in your most comfortable cushion, freezing every time you cat approached him for a caress. Imagine you later found out that the first guy didn't like cats at all but only kept Sissy company to impress you, whereas the second guy didn't care either way but he couldn't be bothered to play with Sissy simply because he was afraid to get cat fur on his silk jacket. So which one of these guys would be more in your good graces? Yeah that's what I thought.

Some guys have leisure activities they enjoy so much, they would probably trade it in for their day job if they could. Say your date enjoys the occasional game of football, you could show your interest by going to the game with him. Just knowing you are on the bleachers cheering him on is enough to make any man three feet taller. Try not to be too much of a stereotypical "girl." You should be able to let your hair down, tell jokes, watch sports, play video games or even play good ol' poker with him and try to enjoy the things that he enjoys. That's a very flattering compliment and he won't miss it.

The best way you can show interest in a man is to develop the art of genuinely listening to him. Even if you are a regular chatter-box with ideas popping into your head a mile a minute, you might want to dial back the incessant chatter and listen to him with every fibre of your being. There is something about being at the receiving end of so much unpretentious attention that makes people want to reciprocate. Being a good listener is never a bad idea especially since you are still at the brink of starting something with this guy. It makes him relax and reveal things about himself to you. Trust me, you want to know as much as you can about a man before you give your heart to him because the thing about destructive relationships is most people stay in them well past the expiry date because they don't know how to just take back their hearts and leave.

Show interest in a man alright but do not go overboard with this. When you first meet a man, try to keep the conversation light and hearty; it does not have to be overtly sexual either. Avoid talking about work, family, religion for too long, if at all. You should keep you earlier interactions fun, short and sweet;

it is often more memorable that way and it makes him want to discover more about you.

Every human being is not immune to genuine, sincere interest so the next time you want to catch a man's attention, be sure to toe this line.

CHAPTER SIX

Dare To Be Different

Whoever told you that different is bad is not your friend—either that or they are so ignorant, it's a wonder they have survived this long in our world.

Fashion trends are a good thing but sometimes they can be bad too. I have never understood some people's fascination with looking just like a clone of everyone else. Dare to be different! Stand out from the crowd and that's how you get noticed.

Don't let other people define you; decide on who you want to be and go for it.

In today's world, being different could be something as simple as having a signature look. For instance, while everyone else is tripping over cocktail dresses made just so, a woman in Ankara fabric cleverly sewn into the most amazing cocktail dress ever would stand out without even trying.

If there is anything anyone should take to heart, it's that we should all be originals. Forcing yourself into a role society has pre-destined for you also forces alarming mediocrity upon you. Being part of the mould means you get lost in the shuffle of things and that's really no way to attract attention.

Consider this: you are already unique anyway with a perspective all your own that no one else has but unless you are willing to colour outside the lines, you may never pick up your crayon at all.

To be perfectly honest, it is a whole lot easier to just sit back and go with the flow because sometimes being different can feel like you are moving against the tide but there are a few things you should consider. In all my years of sojourn on earth, I have seen even the most confirmed, foot-loose and fancy-free bachelor fall fast and hard for a woman and rush her straight to the altar before she even has a chance to draw breath after saying yes. In every single case, the men always said, "She's different from every girl I have ever met".

Honestly I never met a man or woman for that matter who fell in love because the other person was just like everyone else. Being different means you get noticed for your uniqueness; it means you are an original in a world of clones; it is a refreshing change and everyone will want to get closer to you.

Listen if the price you have to pay for being different is that some people would not like you or appreciate you, then good because not everyone appreciates a Van Gogh. Never apologize for being who you are; just embrace it and celebrate your own individuality. That often means that you will end up as a person who knows exactly what they want out of life and how to get it. Of course as soon as you learn to love and celebrate your own individuality, people will be attracted into your life who will do the same too.

You don't want to be common or pedestrian now do you? I think the courage to be different lies in knowing your own worth from the outset. The beauty of being different is that it makes you much more memorable and that much harder to forget and yes, that's exactly the kind of attention you want to attract from a man. I mean wouldn't you like to be the girl he cannot stop thinking about?

Here are a few practical tips to help you achieve the originality inside of you:

1.   Own your style

If you are like most people, your style is dictated by the current trend in pop culture and while that's okay, the truth remains that you will never really appreciate your creativity or your own self-worth for that matter until you learn to own your style. In essence, never wear something just because someone else is wearing it. Try to get good quality clothes in unique pieces; wearing mass produced clothes means you could run into a twin everywhere from the salon to the boardroom and trust me, you do *not* want that. Be your own role model when it comes to fashion; decide what works for you and try it out. Don't be afraid to try new things. Most people who break out of a mould prefer to go for timeless and classy pieces when it comes to fashion and that's often such a hit because you can't go wrong with timeless. Some prefer edgy and modern too. The key is find what works for you; choose what suits your personal style best.

You can determine your personal style in one easy step: just pick up at least three old fashion magazines. Flip through and cut out pictures of every style or clothing that you think looks amazing. When you are done, arrange the picture son a clipboard and look at it. I am willing to bet it all leans towards a particular style doesn't it? Well in that case, that's your personal style. Whether its casual, classy, old money, new age, whatever really; you can make it work if you are true to yourself and your own preferences rather than following the crowd.

2.   Do what you really want to do not what everyone else is doing

If your idea of a perfect date is fishing for rare amphibians in a creek then you should just go ahead and suggest it to your date. Two things will happen; he may decide he doesn't like your 'weirdness' and run for the hills after date number one, or he may find your strange fascination so cute and different and unforeseen that he will be drawn back to you like a moth to a flame.

In scenario one, do not feel bad or even mourn the loss of his companionship even for a second because in my view, you just dodged a bullet. A person who sees the real you and does not like what he sees is not worth your time or even a drop of your tears. Here's why: If you end up dating him, you will always be exhausted trying to keep up the pretence, trying to be someone else. The moment the real you starts to show its face, he will either accuse you of changing and walk away or he will just freak out and still walk away. Either way, you lose after you have invested time, energy and emotions into that relationship.

3.   Don't take different to the extreme

At this point, I am guessing you know that I applaud individuality as much as the next person but there are extremes to that behaviour you don't want to go close to. For instance, it is okay to be that girl who prefers to be as blunt as can be. However if you start crossing the line from blunt into rude, you will just push people away and end up lonely. Different is good when it means you are true to yourself and stand out from the crowd. Different is not good when it involves committing a crime or hurting someone else.

4.   Spend time with yourself

A little alone time, with just your thoughts for company may be just what the doctor ordered. It often means you can let your thoughts fly free and let yourself meditate on where your life is going. Being different means you have to know who you really are and what you really want. You cannot do that if you are so busy rushing about in a noisy world that you end up drowning out your inner consciousness. Besides if you learn not to neglect yourself, you will find it hard to settle for a relationship where your partner is neglectful.

5.   Listen to music you like and pick up hobbies that interest you

So you never out-grew your childhood hobby of picking rocks, who cares? Go ahead and pick enough rocks to fill the whole of Texas if that makes you happy. Being different means being true to yourself and if you can achieve this, there is an automatic self-assurance that comes with it which means you will automatically appear put together and let me tell you, there are few things as attractive and sexy as a woman who has self-assurance.

You don't have to listen to Taylor Swift just because your girlfriends are all gushing over her. If Michael Jackson does it for you, then by all means listen to his music.

6.   Let your mischievous side out

Girls are always meant to be cute and sweet and charming; or at least that is what some of us think. It's okay to have a naughty side too so long as it doesn't involve playing cruel tricks on people. Being mischievous means you have this zing, this unexpected side. Some guys may be prone to taking life too seriously or even to acting as if the entire world is at their feet. A bit of mischief sans idol worship is just the ticket to bring them back to earth with an audible crash. Being mischievous means you are comfortable in your own skin and it also means you consider him human enough to treat him like a normal person. Some guys may have achieved so much in life that they come to expect women to worship them; you do not want to be that girl, trust me. So go ahead and tease him, play naughty but cute tricks on him and laugh at him and with him. Laugh at yourself too while you are at it, just for the sake of balance.

Besides, being mischievous means he always has to be on his toes around you and in my book, that's a far cry from boring. He will keep coming back for more delicious and exciting torture at your hands. And yes, you will be entertained too especially if he is someone who knows how to hold his own with you.

7.   Don't apologize for your beliefs

So you are a woman who believes in God or Santa Claus or equality of the sexes or even the tooth fairy; be proud of whatever belief you have and never apologize for it especially if you honestly believe in that. So long as you are not crazy, stick to your beliefs and hold it dear.

It does not make you opinionated mind, it just means you are not a pushover and that you are willing to stand up for what you believe in.

PART THREE
HOW TO KEEP HIS
ATTENTION

So you have got his attention; now how do
you keep it? This Part discusses ways to keep
his attention on you for the long haul.

CHAPTER SEVEN

Compliment Him Always

Men really are less complicated than most women realize. Ladies sometimes make the mistake of thinking that men are indifferent and impervious to compliments. In truth though, unless he's *Jabba the Hunt*, he probably enjoys getting his ego massaged with sincere compliments as much as the next person.

Honest, sincere compliments have an even longer-lasting effect on guys than they do on ladies. Women are usually thrilled to be recipients of great compliments, and let's face it, most women get compliments all the time from their boss, their friends, co-workers, their neighbours; you name it. Strangely though, most men rarely get complimented for their achievements, looks and what have you. Society seems to have adopted this approach of expecting men to suck it up when they have problems, roll with it when they are stressed, and count every achievement as just par for the course.

Just in case you didn't know, compliments are often a stepping stone to a happy, flirty conversation. Even if you just met a man, a warm, sincere compliment could be an easy way to strike up a conversation.

Compliments make anyone happy; you should know that, since I'm willing to bet that you've probably been on the receiving end of a few compliments yourself. So you should understand why they would have a positive effect on a guy. But even better, with guys, sincere compliments make them remember you and the compliment for a long time.

So whether you've just met him or you are already on the first or second date, you will grab his attention with carefully, well-timed compliments. Note to the wise though; fawning, insincere blarney will get you nowhere. Unless he's a rock-star and you're a groupie, he can probably spot insincere flattery from a mile away — yes, despite how clueless you like to think guys are.

Now compliments do work like a charm with guys, but some compliments tend to go a long way more than others. The trick is in knowing what to compliment as well as how to do it. For instance, complimenting his bod would make him feel good yes, but unless he's a physical trainer or just looking to get in your pants, crowing incessantly about his incredible biceps may start to wear thin after a while.

Here are some tips on how to compliment him and make him think of you more:

1.   Compliment his driving skills

Unless you live under a rock, you probably know that guys are really all about electronics, gadgets, and engines; am I getting warm yet? Gadgets are irresistible to every male of the specie, from chubby-cheeked little boys to handsome dudes in their prime to septuagenarians with nothing but fading memories of a happy past. Men have always and will always love being behind the wheels of a powerful car or even a sexy, powerful Vespa because that's just how they are built. It's the same thing that makes them competitive; and it's the same thing that makes them zone out in front of a television set watching 22 guys chase a ball around a field; it's the same reason they'd rather tinker with the dishwasher than take it in for repairs.

He'll probably never admit it, but every guy, on some level, thinks he's a better driver than just about everyone else. It's the competitive spirit; and to an extent, it's also the reason road-rage is more common than we would like.

But the good news is, you can use this to etch yourself more firmly onto his mind. The next time he executes a particularly smooth manoeuvre behind the wheel, try to tamp down on your first instinct to lecture him on the values of driving like a snail and do compliment him on his classy driving skills.

Speaking of driving, I should probably point out at this point that nagging him about taking a wrong turn is a definite no-no and a buzz kill.

2. Chivalry and principles

Chivalry is fast-becoming a lost art so if your man is sensitive enough to pull out your chair, offer you his arm when you are trying to navigate a particularly rough flight of stairs in heels, or just hold the door open for you, you should make certain to compliment him for having great manners.

Most twenty-first century men are sadly lacking in common courtesies towards the fairer sex. So when you find yourself in the presence of a man thoughtful enough to extend any form of chivalry towards you, be sure to flash him your cutest smile compliment his chivalry.

Men with principles are sadly fewer than we would like to admit. A lot of men have little or no scruples so when you do find yourself in the presence of a man who does have such principles, be sure to compliment him on that. The fact that you recognize and appreciate his principles will make him proud of himself. Also, the fact that you are a girl who appreciates a principled man would stick in his brain. In a man's world, you must be a principled girl yourself which is why you could have appreciated that in him. See?

Your appreciation encourages him to keep doing that and frankly, you can't go wrong.

3.   His clothes and tastes

While I'm willing to admit that guys are not necessarily as fashion-conscious as ladies, (I mean let's face it, he would only just come off as a narcissist), it does not hurt at all to let him know you think his choice of apparel is a definite winner. Men love power so go right ahead and tell him his clothes make him look powerful. I remember once I told a date I loved it when men wore white on white because I thought it made them look powerful. He just shrugged nonchalantly; he wasn't wearing a stitch of white at the time. To my surprise though, he wore white on white at least twice every week for the next year. I ran into him three years later and he was all in white; it was the darnest thing!

See what I mean? Sometimes it's not just the compliment they never forget, it's you!

Some men are hopelessly colour blind (some would argue that *all* men are) but some men do know how to combine colours. Compliment him on this if he does so. If he also happens to be a refined gentleman with impeccable taste, please do not hold back on the compliments; let him know you noticed and you like it. Evidence of his good taste could be in everything from the way he keeps his house, to the kind of wine he orders at dinner. In whatever way he shows impeccable taste, he really is trying to impress you. praise him and let him know you were impressed; it's the only way to make certain he wants to impress you again in the future.

4.   Ask his opinion, advice, help

Men are natural fixers, so if you have a problem, don't be afraid to ask for his help or assistance. The mere fact that you valued his opinion or wisdom enough to ask will leave him on cloud nine. Plus, the fact that you are turning to him for guidance does wonders for his protective instinct. Do not be surprised if he finds it hard to leave your side.

Sometimes asking for advice is not just about him but about you too. Knowing you have a listening ear kinda puts things in perspective doesn't it? It encourages you to also look at your problem from another angle. It's also a good chance for you to confirm that he has a good head on his shoulders.

Men are naturally wired to be protective and society doesn't help much either: remember all those times Mum chided your brother to look out for you at school even though you were two years older than him and probably half a foot taller? Exactly.

Most men, the good ones that is, believe they have been placed in the natural role of protector and provider. In today's world though, that is a kind of tall order to fill when you consider that most women are happily independent and more than capable of fending for themselves in the big bad world, thank you very much. Some psychologists have suggested is that the effect is that most men are secretly at a loss as to what to do with themselves since the roles have been so significantly shifted; and is it any wonder more and more men are ending up in therapy? Well I don't know how true that theory is, but the fact remains that making a man know you need him is one of the best compliments you can pay him. Don't believe me? Ask your boyfriend to hang the lights next Christmas. Feel free to chip in the fact that he is so much taller and stronger than you are, and would be able to reach the top of the tree much better; then sit back and watch him tackle the task as though he were saving dainty little you from World War III.

5.   Compliment his wit and intellect

No one likes to be the stereotypical dumb blonde so beauty and no brains is never a winning combination for ladies or guys. If he has unusual smarts, do not pretend not to notice. Compliment him on that as sincerely as possible. It will show you appreciate him and make him walk just a few inches taller because let us face it, who does not like to be admired?

If he says something funny, let loose and have a good laugh at that one; I promise your face won't crack even if you had Botox. Guys love it when they can make a girl laugh because few emotions connect people faster than humour and everyone knows that. Most guys would even tell you that they like it when a girl laughs at their jokes just like most girls would tell you that one of the reasons they love a guy is because he makes them laugh.

I think being able to laugh at a guy's jokes, and actually laughing, is the greatest compliment you can possibly pay to his wit and humour. I mean let's face it, telling him how funny he is whilst your face is carved in stone is kinda counterproductive isn't it?

6. Compliment his physique and let him know you are not the only one who has noticed

This one is for you and him; compliment his bod but don't go overboard with it because even if he does look like a Greek god, you do not want to come across as trying too hard. Now here's the good part: if you happen to notice every other woman checking him out, lean in close to him and point it out. Know why this is for both of you? Leaning in close creates a sense of intimacy that lets him get a whiff of your amazing scent and also helps remind you that even though other women are checking him out, you are the one on his arm. Plus, the mere fact that you are not threatened by other women's attention towards him makes you so much more interesting and he would want to get to know you some more just to figure out what makes you tick.

This one is a bit tricky though, especially down the line. If you overdo it, he may develop a swelled head and a narcissist tendency;

compliment him but keep it simple. Don't become all gushy and adoring because he is not a celebrity and you are not a groupie. And hey, even if he *is* a celebrity, if you overstress his awesomeness you may create a new monster — the unfaithful kind.

The awesome thing about complimenting a guy's physique is that you don't always have to say a word, especially if you are the shy type. Just give him a good, long, appreciative stare; I'm thinking the kind of intense, hungry look you would reserve for an ice cream on a particularly hot day. If he doesn't get hot under the collar from that one, then I don't know what he is made of, but it certainly ain't flesh and blood!

7.   Brag

No, this is not the carte blanche you have been waiting for to start bragging about yourself. Brag about him! Brag to your friends, his friends and everyone else who will listen; bonus points if you do this in front of him. He may blush and act like he is embarrassed but in truth, you have just paid him an amazing compliment and he won't be forgetting it or you in a hurry. He will be so pleased, especially if all the stuff you were bragging about are true; exaggerated perhaps, but true nevertheless.

The thing about compliments though, be careful not to put him on a pedestal like he can do no wrong. He is human so if he starts to get too full of himself, feel free to take him down a peg or two with gentle teasing and humour. The fact that you can tease him, encourages him not to take himself too seriously and he will end up trying harder to prove himself.

CHAPTER EIGHT

Put the Brake On

When a man likes you, he is usually in a hurry to sample all you have got to offer; and I don't just mean your body, but yes, that *is* a part of it. A man who likes you will be in a hurry to get to know all there is to know about you, and yes that can be very exciting and can easily go to your head. The flip side though is that if you don't slow him down, he quickly loses interest. How do I put this? If you fill his throat with too much ... you, he will barf and throw you right out.

Okay first things first; if he's talking about white picket fences and getting married when you have only been on the first date, I would advise you wipe the goofy grin right off your face and run for the hills. And yes, I don't care if you're pushing fifty! Any man with good intentions would naturally be inclined to take things a bit slower to see if you are a good fit. When it comes to relationships, slow and steady does win the race. If he simply starts tossing matrimony left and right, he may only be looking for a quick route to your panties.

1.   Get in some time away from him

This is the part where I tell you to play hard to get but without overdoing it. Make sure you get in some time away from him; that change of perspective may help you see things more clearly and frankly, the fact that you are not always around him, will help your case — a lot.

Being away from him every now and then means you give him time to miss you and trust me, that is not a bad idea at all. Sometimes it takes missing a person to realise just how important they are to us. Also, you could use the opportunity to reconnect with your friends. Most people make the mistake of inadvertently cutting off friends when they start seeing someone they like, but in my book, that is a definite no-no. The reason is, if you have no other friends, you inadvertently make him your whole world— and pretty quickly too.

Also, what if the relationship progresses and ends in disaster further down the line? You have no one to talk to about it and no one to help you pick up the pieces. If that isn't sad, I don't know what is. In most cases, people remain in relationships they don't like because they don't have a support system or they fear the inevitable loneliness that would follow cutting off the one friend they do have. Don't be that girl. Keep your friends around you because more often than not, they were there before he was and most times, they will be there after he leaves.

Get in some 'me time' too while you are at it because the truth is that sometimes it is so easy to get swept up in the romance of a new relationship that you end up losing yourself in the process. Take some time to let the dust settle and examine this guy as objectively as possible. Does he have some personality traits you need to make excuses for? Because if he does, you should keep in mind that personality traits do not change; not really. These are the things that crop up further down the line and end up ruining your mascara.

Go away on vacation if you must and meet new people, see new places; it's exciting and good for you and your relationship. Knowing you are sunning yourself on some exotic beach probably meeting a person or five, would make the seat of his trousers smoke. It also means you have managed to maintain your independence. Your life is not defined by him because he is a part of your life not your whole life.

2.   Go on group dates

Speaking of friends, utilise yours by inviting them to join both of you on dates. It's a great way to meet new people and to introduce him to your circle of friends and vice versa. At the same time, the large group of people acts as a buffer which means you get to relax and avoid super-charged intimate scenes. Group dates mean you all can go to the movies rather than having an intimate dinner for two. It takes the pressure off, makes it seem like you are just hanging out as opposed to being in a serious relationship; plus it makes you seem less desperate and puts him firmly in the position of chaser if you suggested the group date.

A word of advice though; if he's just meeting your friends for the first time, he's virtually the new kid on the block. If he's interested in you, he will most likely be watching to ascertain your relationship with the other guys in the group. You don't want to give him the wrong impression by acting all lovey-dovey with someone else in the group. If you do, chances are he would back off in a hurry if he doesn't want to step on any toes.

3. Now would be a good time to whip the career card out of your back pocket

No you don't have to morph into a workaholic overnight; just learn to start seeing less of him and more of your office for the time being.

You could simply tell him you are going to be busy for the next four weeks and may not be able to see him during the weekdays, except the weekends. That's reasonable and plausible enough and hey, you know what they say about absence making the heart grow fonder.

Although it would be in extremely bad form if you cut down on your time with him and used the opportunity to see some other guy.

4. Make post-date plans

No not with him, with other friends. Knowing you have to get to other friends after your lunch or dinner together keeps you honest. In fact, you could schedule your meetings with him for lunch as opposed to dinner.

Knowing you have somewhere to run to means the chances of ending up together in your bed or his are so very slim they are practically non-existent.

Also, just to earn his respect further, turn down sudden date invitations; if he wants the pleasure of your company for an outing over the weekend, he should make the effort to call you at the latest on Thursday. Do *not* accept to go out with him on Saturday if he only just called the same Saturday; do not accept a date for Friday night if he could not call to plan before Wednesday. Politely say that you already made plans. You don't have to suggest an alternate date though; let that come from him. Just say something vague like, "Perhaps some other time".

Knowing you are busy and likely hanging out with some other dude puts him on his toes and makes him more serious in his pursuit of you because now, he senses hat he could lose you. It also puts him on notice that you are not going to wait around. If he wants to spend time with you, he should be able to show serious effort. It's also your own way of ensuring you are not at his beck and call.

5.   Let him know you don't want to rush

It's okay to have him on the same page as yourself so he does not misread your signals, assume you are not interested and back off altogether. Relationships are fun if you take the time to savour every stage; do not let him rush you before you even have time to get your sea legs. Whether it's sex or meeting his best friends or his parents, if you are not ready to take the next step in the relationship, you are not; and don't let anyone arm-twist you into something you are not ready for. If he is the right person, he would wait until your feelings have caught up to his. You want a man who is understanding enough to respect your reservations and not one who mocks them and makes you feel as though you are wrong to have reservations in the first place.

Knowing you are not in such a doggone hurry to take the relationship further will win you his respect; whether he admits it or not. Plus he will be more careful about the way treats you since obviously your life does not revolve around him.

At the same time, don't take forever to figure it out or he may think you don't have interest in him anymore and he would probably go away for good.

CHAPTER NINE

Control the Goodies

Alright don't kill the messenger, but the truth is, Mum may have been right when she asked you to keep it in your pants as much as possible. And yes, Granny was also onto something when she admonished you not to 'put out' before a guy had shown you any real commitment.

In today's world, sexuality is a whole lot more relaxed and accepted than it used to be and frankly, some men are so completely turned on by a woman who knows what she wants and goes for it. But the fact remains that if you are into 'putting out' before the wine has so much as dried up from the wineglass on your first date, you may have an uphill task getting any man to commit to you.

Now I realize that this may offend every single one of your feminist sensibilities but the truth is, men love a challenge, and if you aren't the least bit challenging, he quickly loses interest and moves on to the next available … person.

Have you ever watched lions hunt? Well if you are reading this, it means you're pretty much alive, so I am willing to guess you haven't — at least not personally anyway. Regardless, the fact remains that no predator is ever attracted to dead meat; they had much rather move in for the kill on vital, fleeing prey.

Sex is a big deal for most people and the fact that you are one of such people really does not make you gauche or naive. Truth be told, with the lessened rate of morality in the system he would probably appreciate the fact that you are not anxious to hop into bed with the first guys who asks. But being a guy, he would prefer if you gave him a booty call every night for a year with no strings attached but the truth is, sex creates an attachment; it's just the way most women are wired.

Sex could create a false sense of intimacy which is why you should not introduce it too early into your relationship. Most women have sex too early and end up becoming clingy because it's obvious they are more vested in the relationship than he is.

When a man's attention is fixed on you for the right reasons, holding off on sex will just help the anticipation build up. Although if you are doing this, you might want to make certain to let him know that you are very much interested in him but sex is just not on the cards for now. If you are careless enough to hold off on sex whilst keeping him completely in the dark as to whether you like him or not for a long time, you stand the unfortunate chance of making him think you are leading him on a string.

Holding off on sex —— or cutting down if you are already having it —— is one sure-fire way to make sure he does not get bored of you before he has had a chance to discover how amazing you really are and fall in ,love with you.

Men are always going to want sex anyway they can get it, but sex is never going to make them stay with you. So if you were nursing some mistaken belief that sexing him up is going to make him want to stick with you, guess again.

Don't get me wrong it's alright to seduce him, be naughty every now and then to get his juices flowing in the right direction. But just make certain that you are having sex with him for you; because you want to and not because you think it is going to bind him to you. The only person that's going to be feeling bound by new emotions courtesy of sex is probably you.

Also, while we are on the subject, the popular "Have sex on the third date rule" is just wrong. Third date? Really? What do you know about this man by the third date? Wait to have sex until you are completely sure of his intentions. Sit back, tuck in your feet and let him chase you. The mere fact that you are in the role of relaxed observer makes it easier for you to spot red flags in his personality you would not have noticed otherwise. For instance, a man who is insanely jealous and possessive is not a good thing, contrary to popular opinion. In fact studies have shown that most of such men end up becoming violent towards their partner for some perceived infidelity or encouragement of other men's advances.

CHAPTER TEN

Be Independent

First off, you could be fun, amazing, intelligent, sexy as all get out and every man's dream girl and a guy could still lose interest in you faster than you could say Rumpelstiltskin. Sadly, it won't be because you were not good enough but because you were just too much for him.

People often say 'Get a life' with as much sarcasm as they can muster up but in truth, it's actually good advice.

If you have managed to snag the attention of a really good guy, you don't want to screw things up by turning up like a bad penny every time he turns around and carrying out surveillance on his home and office. Every man values his privacy and once he begins to sense that you are constantly invading it, he may start to avoid you, even without meaning to.

You can be the girl who is independent of her man despite how crazy she is about him; you can be the girl he calls in the middle of the day to say how much he misses her; you can be the woman who has his attention and commands his respects. All you have to do — literally — is get a life by trying out some of these steps below:

1.   Get new friends

As you get older, you inevitably lose some old friends; if you don't replace them with new ones, you end up lonely soon; it is basic Math really. People move away, people grow apart, and people just plain stop being friends with each other. Make efforts to meet new people and include them in your circle of friends; it's how you make sure you have a social life.

Sometimes new friends are not so new. They could simply be people with whom you have a passing casual acquaintance whom perhaps you have never spoke to. Go out of your way to do something different with respect to them. For instance, you could send them an email, you could ask them to meet you for lunch, or you could invite them to go with you instead to that charity event you have been thinking of asking your new guy to join you on.

You could easily convert mere acquaintances into friends by showing genuine interest in them. You don't have to approach them seeking favours, but you could approach them with wonderful ideas guaranteed to make their lives better. They would follow you in no time and don't be surprised if you strike up a friendship as a result.

If you are on the shy side, making friends can be almost physically painful. Well feel free to ask for their telephone numbers and sometimes invite them to hang out with you and your other friends— assuming you have other friends. Also, you could be the one staving off every offer of friendship without realizing it. The next time a co-worker asks you to hang out with a group of friends for drinks after work, try not to mumble into your shirt collar that you 'already have plans' especially when those plans are nothing more pressing than you in your pajamas holding a bowl of popcorn and scrolling through Netflix.

2.   Get a new hobby or resuscitate an old one

Hobbies keep you young and fresh, put the spring back in your step and make you smile. Having great hobbies that keep you busy is a sure way to make certain that you do not turn your relationship into a whiny, needy affair where one person has all the power.

Some people take up lifestyle challenges; for instance, nothing keeps you busier than say a 30 days challenge involving chatting up at least five strangers a day. you could also try taking up yoga, Pilates, kick-boxing or even good old Tae Kwan Do.

3.   Join a club

Take up a new cause and watch yourself spring into action. Clubs, charities and organizations are always looking for Volunteers. Sign up for a project or two and meet new people as well as interact with several persons. Being able to volunteer for a worthy cause will also make you even more interesting to him which means you can talk about your day when you meet rather than just sitting and staring at him in awe while he talks about how he conquered the world.

If charity is not your cup of tea — although seriously I don't get why it wouldn't be — you could try to join groups like professional associations, religious groups, cooking classes, design groups, you get the drift. Just look for a group of people who have a common passion with you and join them. And if you cannot find a group that mirrors your passion, well take the initiative and start one! The rush from that alone will keep you vital, young and enhance your magnetism no end.

There is something about getting a life that keeps people unable to compromise their values, standards and goals. It gives you a feeling of self-wroth and means you are less inclined to call your significant other every other minute during the day. Keeping busy is good for you, your relationship and in fact your health.

So even if you are in between jobs at the moment, try one of the above and get a life; it will just give him more opportunities to miss you and make him cherish you the more. Just step on out of your comfort zone and go get a life!

The simple rule of thumb is, be fun, in ways that men think are fun. This rule of attraction seems simple enough, but so many girls get it wrong. Be driven, focused and determined; hang out at sports bars with him every now and then and while you are at it, make certain you let him know through subtle clues that while you like him well enough, he is not the centre of your universe. He'll want you even more then.

CHAPTER ELEVEN

Become Friends with His Friends

Men are more easily influenced by other men than they like to admit. Come on you know the way you care what your girlfriends think of him? He does care what his own friends think of you too so you might want to make a good impression. No I have not asked you to bend over backwards just to be accommodating nor have I asked you to stop being yourself just to make them happy. But you do need to be nice.

If a man's friends think you are all that, you bet he would think the same too and hold on to you just a tad more because hey, his friends are competition too; if they think you are hot, so would other guys and he knows it.

One sure way to keep a man's attention is to know how to get along with his friends and make them like you. If he always has to defend you to them or explain why you are so uppity, he may soon start to view your flaws through their eyes.

Men generally tend to act different towards the woman in their life when their friends are around. You should learn to expect and overlook that but please never overlook outright disrespect.

Luckily, unless he's from Krypton, a man's friends are usually just as human as he is which means there are a thousand and one ways you could work it to keep his attention by making his friends like you.

1.   Never try to take him away from them

This is *numero uno* for good reason. If a man's friends are uncomfortable around you because they think you are trying to steal their friend or make him unhappy then you have a bit of a problem. More often than not, they were his buddies before the idea of you was even conceived in his mind so to their way of thinking; they were there first. It may sound juvenile, but human nature being what it is, what do you really expect? They would hardly welcome you with open arms if you obviously resent all the time he spends in their company.

This is the part where I tell you to resist the urge to plan a date during the NBA finals and try *hard* — yes grit your teeth if you must — not to keep calling when they are on a guys' night out.

In fact, if he does suggest cancelling on guys' night out, feign an engagement yourself; he will respect your independence and chances are, he will spend all night thinking about you and come flying back to you as soon as he can.

The fact that you can give him space and breathing room means they can't give him flack about it later. They will respect you for not being clingy and needy and you will be much better off.

In fact, sometimes, do initiate their time together. For instance, you could get them surprise tickets to the game and a six-pack for the road trip. He will fall for you just a little more and so will they.

2.   Never put him down in front of them

Okay I know he can be really, really, really annoying when he puts his mind to it, but try never to fight with him in front of his friends. And by fight, I do mean everything from verbal abuses to fisticuffs — although if you are in a relationship where the pair of you ever do come to fisticuffs, his friends are not the deal-breaker from where I'm sitting. Get out fast and perhaps you should both get some therapy while you are at it.

Fighting with a man in front of his friends is a very bad idea. Men have fragile egos as I am sure you have heard a time or five and the mere fact that you are pissed doesn't mean you should let fly at him in front of his buddies. He will feel humiliated and they will definitely pull him aside the first chance they get and tell him why they think you are bad for him. They will never believe you are the right kind of girl for him.

If a man's friends write you off, you might as well pack up your bags because even if he keeps standing up for you, down the line, you are going to have mega problems.

So yes, the next time he checks out the plunging neckline of your waitress while the pair of you are hanging out with his friends, keep the 'Seriously?' to yourself until you have a moment alone! And even then, try not to bash his head in with a rolling pin. If you are mean to him in private, even if he stays with you, he is bound to tell them about it and they will soon start to detest you and badmouth you which brings you right back to square one.

3. Never put them down in front of him

Okay I will be the best to admit that this seems to be something of a tall order, especially if his friends *deserve* to be put down a little. I mean you could genuinely feel that they do not have his best interests at heart or that they are a terrible influence on him but you do not want to come out guns blazing with all the finesse of a Mafian warlord. Criticizing a guy's friends to him are as tricky as pointing out his flaws and whether you have been dating for two years or two months, it's not an easy call.

Try now and then to speak highly to him about them but only do this in their absence. Trust me, as eager as you are for him to like you, he is more eager for them to like you so he will be sure to report back to them the wonderful things you do say about them.

If you keep harping on their faults, he may start feeling the need to separate you from them and maybe even to take sides. They may win eventually; in fact more often than not, when it comes to picking sides, they often do win.

Now while you are telling him good, funny things about his friends, be careful not to overdo it or he may start to think there is something more going on and that is the last thing you want because the problems that would arise would be something else. Essentially, you *would* be coming between them in a way that is dangerous to end your relationship and get you black-listed in all their collective books — for life!

4.   Brag about him

This is a reversal of the rule on how you should never talk him down in front of his friends. Bragging about him means you think he sets the sun and his friends are bound to pick up on this, especially if you are sincerely honest about it. When they start teasing each other or ribbing him in particular, stick up for him. But don't sound angry as that would be bound to ruin the good camaraderie. Just laugh and tell them how confident you are that your man is gonna whip their butts at Play Station III. He will feel good inside and so will they. Knowing you love and respect their friend means they are gonna treat you right too.

5.   Think of them as your own friends

Talk to them and find out what they like or hate. No you don't have to hide who you are and pretend to be Goody Two Shoes but you do have to make an effort to be nice and to understand why he likes to hang out with them. Engage in friendly arguments with them every now and then and make sure you don't nod like a lizard and pretend to agree with every single thing they say. Just because you have to be nice does not mean you have to be afraid of them.

If one of them does something you don't like, feel free to tell him about it as gently and respectfully as possible.

I will give you fair warning though, your likes and dislikes may be completely different from theirs but that does not have to be a problem. You could learn from them and even teach them a thing or two. Trust me it helps them to see him getting along well with you.

In the same vein of thinking of them as your own friends, you might want to invite them to come hang out with you guys every now and then but make certain that you do not do this when he is trying to plan a special date night.

In fact when both of you do go out alone and you know you will be returning to his house or theirs, feel free to order take-out for them. Your boyfriend may grumble or say that you do not have to do that, but secretly, he will be pleased that you were so thoughtful towards his friends. This will definitely earn you scores in their good books too. Plus, you should also be just as nice to them when your boyfriend is not there. Thinking of them as your own friends makes them that much easier to stomach.

Remembering things about them like their birthday, their first date with a girl they like, an interview or even their row with their boss will score you very, very, high points and they will be raving about what a 'great gal' you are in no time at all.

6. Dial back the Public Display of Affection (PDA)

Yes I know you love him, he loves you, kiss-kiss. But when his friends are with both of you, you will just make them uncomfortable with PDA. Besides, getting too touchy-feely in front of other people may seem romantic to you, but to them, it would just come across as rude and even vulgar. The occasional kiss atop his head or peck on his cheek is very much acceptable in whatever company you may find yourselves; but taking it a step further and pouring on the touches is just going to make everyone uncomfortable. Boyfriend dearest may also be uncomfortable with this whether he admits it or not.

Worse, if his friends are all single — as in no spouse, significant other, or relationship of any sort — you French kissing him from lips to chest in their presence is going to be a little on the nose don't you think?

7.   Bring the feast

Guys love food, and it's not exactly trade secret. If you can bring some food along for him and his friends every now and then, you may be sure you won't lose out. In fact, they will adore you all the more and never let him say a bad word about you.

You don't have to prepare a five-course meal or any such thing mind; just simply grabbing cookies or throwing together some light meal and you are good. Lateefah Drake2 said she saved her marriage with this little trick. Her husband was drifting; she could see it in the way he hung out more with the guys night after night after night. The clever woman calmly invited all his friends for a game night at their place and put out loads of sandwiches and of course, beer. The night was such a huge success, his friends started laying into him every time he so much as upset her.

The morale of the story? In today's world the way to a man's heart is still food, whether he is your boyfriend or boyfriend's friend. So stock up on food and a six-pack the next time you want to knock their socks off. A dinner where you play hostess is not a bad idea either, but since it is so formal, you should probably wait on that one until you are seriously in a relationship; at the very least eight months to a year into the relationship.

---

2   Not her real name

But as with all good things, you don't want to go overboard with this because if they get too comfortable with this, they will end up resenting you when you don't bring something to eat. And let's face it, you are his girlfriend not his Mummy so do not let your role get confused.

8. Bring your friends

It can't hurt to introduce your single friends to his, as they may hit it off. But be careful not to overtly match-make because if it doesn't work out in the end, you don't want one of his friends resenting you for being so happy when he is so miserable.

When there is a group event like a picnic, just mention casually that you will be bringing a hot friend or two and on that day, follow through. If they hit it off, credit goes to you. See?

CHAPTER TWELVE

Let Go of Jealousy

Most men have the roving eye — sad but true; and no, I am not making excuses for them. But when it comes to keeping a man's attention firmly fixed on you, jealousy is not your friend. Jealousy is a normal emotion especially when you think someone else is moving in on your partner. Jealousy however is often counter-productive especially when it moves beyond the realm of reason into an angry need to assert control.

Jealousy over a man will just seem ridiculous and awkward if you give into it when you have not defined your relationship or made certain of what exactly your place is in his life. I mean, even I would have to admit you would look very ridiculous if you started acting jealous because a friendly waitress batted her eyes at him on your second date. Come on!

Jealousy often stems from love but in the end, nothing destroys a relationship quite as fast as jealousy. It soon degenerates into one endless vicious cycle of mistrust, unspoken hate, and even revenge. Jealousy can make a sane, placid person crazy; why else do you think the statistics show an alarming number of murders committed by jealous spouses or boyfriends or girlfriends? Most suicides also have foundation in jealousy and even more frightening, they sometimes turn out to be murder-suicides. Jealousy if left unchecked can drive a person so crazy they end up hurting themselves or the one the love or both.

Here are a few reasons why jealousy may be ruining your relationship and causing his attention to drift:

1.   Jealousy cuts off communication

Jealousy is easy to understand when your partner has cheated on you, but the truth is that in such a scenario, you have two choices; either you end the relationship or you learn to deal with your jealousy. Jealousy causes you to hurl ugly accusations around and no matter how justified they may be, you just end up putting him on the defensive and destroying all open channels of communication.

Learn to be guided by your brain and not your heart when the green-eyed monster sits on your shoulder. Calmly discussing through whatever has you bothered will be infinitely more productive than giving in to your instincts and yelling or screaming blue murder.

Put yourself in the other person's shoes; how receptive would you be if you were at the receiving end of anger and accusations? That would put your back up immediately wouldn't it?

So the next time you want to discuss something that makes you jealous, rather than start with the dreaded "We need to talk" or worse, angry screams, try to just say something like, "I seem to be bothered about something and I can't think of anyone I had rather discuss it with than you."

Learn to use your pronouns too; don't say stuff like, "You made me jealous when you were staring at that woman." Say something that removes him from the active and points at you instead like, "I was a bit jealous when I observed you looking at that woman." It's less confrontational and the chances of you talking about it is higher.

2.   It makes you seem insecure

No matter the cause of jealousy, the end result does not look pretty on you; it makes you seem insecure and lacking in self-worth and you really don't want that. Say you are on a date and you catch another girl checking him out, just lean in towards him and tease quietly about how other women in the room applaud your taste.

Men like to be admired, they also like to be in the company of a beautiful, strong, independent woman who knows her place in the world and can hold her own with anyone. Knowing you are completely comfortable in your own element even when he is surrounded by a hundred beautiful women would just make you even more attractive and desirable to him. Men rarely admit it but they usually like women who are independent and able to move through life without needing him to hold their hand every step of the way.

The fact that you are so sure, so secure and so confident will drive him crazy in a good way even if he does not say so. That kind of confidence is also so sexy and hot, and it will firmly cement his attentions on you.

True love never comes about because you were so jealous and possessive that you successfully leashed him to your side. True love comes about when you set someone free and they choose you. it is a damn good feeling knowing he could have gone with a million other women and yet he chose you; and all you had to do was be your lovely, amiable, kick-ass personality, sexy, beautiful, intelligent self.

3.   Jealousy makes you seem controlling and manipulative

This is especially true when you are in a happy relationship where your partner has never strayed not given you cause for worry but your jealous stems from the fact that you are afraid of losing him. In most cases like this, jealousy would be a big problem and may even end up driving him away. Here's why; he starts feeling trapped and then starts feeling as though he has been coerced into something against his will. You don't want that at all.

Jealousy may be your way of possessively guarding what you think belongs to you (picture a little child and its toy) but unfortunately your partner is a living, breathing human being with thoughts, and mind of his own. He won't appreciate being clutched protectively like a toy as though he had no choice in the matter. So loosen your grip. If he stays, he stays, and if he does not, you are a vital, amazing woman anyway; it's his loss.

In any relationship, it is in human nature to want the freedom of choice. Take that away and you have a full scale rebellion on your hands. What I am saying is this, more often than not; jealousy pushes the one you love into cheating on you. So ironically, the very thing you feared the most will have been brought about by your own actions. In that case, why not sit back and enjoy the ride rather than stressing yourself and chasing the wind

Jealousy can be a big turn-off; notice I am not mincing words right now because I want you to get it. It could be a very big turn-off.

Jealousy is not something that can be overcome in one single bound. The first step is to admit that you have a problem and then use patience, self-reflection and persistence to slowly work on flushing the poison of jealousy from your system. Your future relationships will thank you for it, and so will your blood pressure.

Once you realize that he is with you because he wants to be and not because he is under pressure from your jealousy, you should learn to loosen the leash a little or better still, do away with it completely. Your efforts to keep him interested in you and only you may in fact put so much pressure on him that you end up pushing him into the arms of someone else completely.

Your partner is his own person and the tighter you hold onto him, the faster you snuff out his feelings for you. Don't ask me why this is so, it's just one of the ironies of life.

A good way to combat jealousy is with selfishness. Okay it sounds weird, but just go with me for a minute. Your jealousy often stems from obsession with your partner; like you stand to lose the whole world if he walks out. But in truth, if you start to take on more activities and focus more on your own life, that desperate need to hold on to him eases. In fact, most women who have successfully changed tactics ended up being the object of hot, ardent, focused daily pursuit from that very partner. Spend your emotional and intellectual resources more on yourself; build yourself not your resentment and watch your health become an amazingly stable force in your life.

Remember at all times that he is a person; his own person, and not a possession and I think you should be just fine.

Being able to rise above jealousy gives you an added air of maturity that automatically commands his respect. Relationships come and go no matter how much time or otherwise you may have put into it; working with the mindset that the relationship may end one day allows you to relax and just enjoy the time you do have together. I mean, whichever way the cookie crumbles in the end, you want to have happy and fond memories to look back on not screaming matches and hissy fits right?

CHAPTER THIRTEEN

Pace and Lead

Think of relationships as a dance; there are steps, two partners, and measured guidance involved. Have you ever seen someone dance a cotillion? One partner leads the dance to ensure harmony of steps. If both partners try to lead at the same time, they could end up squashing each other's toes all up. There is a tempo to relationships and when you lose track of the rhythm, you could end up with badly bruised toes, an emotional limp, and a broken neck (or in this case, heart).

When you have captured a man's attention, learn to give as good as you get. There are stages in relationships as I believe I have mentioned a time or two and since, more often than not, he does the chasing and wooing, you might want to follow his lead. Men are naturally averse to commitments and if you desire to keep his attention, I am going to take a wild stab and say that commitment is in the cards for you; at least from your own end. If you want to keep his attention on you, you do *not* want to overwhelm him, rather, let the relationship progress as it will. Here are a few ideas for you to keep in mind:

1.　Follow his lead.

Most men are not looking for monogamy or commitment; sad but true. It often grows on them or hits them over the head. But one truth that has remained unchanged is that with men, the harder you try to 'wring an offer from them' or corral them into a monogamous, exclusive relationship, the more they will resist you.

Don't get me wrong, women over time have indeed been wringing offers and corralling to their heart's content but the fine art of subtlety has to be at work so he has little or no idea what you are really doing.

If he is into going out with you three times a week, *never* try to force the issue of making it five times a week; let the idea come from him. You *could* however make him see the benefits of having you by his side more often than not by making yourself scarce on some of those appointed days or making those dates such fun that he will positively be salivating with the need to see you again. In fact, if you play your cards right, he will be the one inviting himself over to dinner at your house and asking to sleep over or some such thing— although of course letting him sleep over without a commitment is definitely out.

Speaking of, never ask to move in. Let the initiative come from him because if you force the issue, he may cave in but once you have a really bad argument, you will discover what he really thinks of you for forcing yourself into his home.

2.   Don't call him a thousand times a day; follow the three call rule

So his phone may be ringing off the hook all day, but make sure those calls are not from you; unless of course you are trying to make sure he waded safely through a blizzard or some such thing.

It's normal to always want to hear the voice of the man you love but frankly constant calls could be an irritant; or worse, they could make him take you for granted. I mean if you are always available at his beck and call, do not be surprised if he ceases to appreciate you as much as you would have otherwise liked him to. Men are unable to appreciate what they can get easily and if your attention is one of those things, you are going to get a lot of emotional bruises for all your trouble. It's the competitive streak all men are born with that makes them always crave a challenge. So if he has to work for every morsel of your time, or work hard to get you to so much as pick up your phone to call him, you may be sure he will cherish every little call you toss his way. In fact, the rarer the better. Just think how special you would feel if he stopped to take your call right in the middle of some power lunch or even while driving.

In the world of relationships, calling is part of the chase. Here's an analogy for you; have you ever heard the male peacock make the mating sound? I am told it is the most annoying sound in the world; but notice *he* does the calling because calling the female is its own form of chase. If you call a man constantly, he will get bored, get lazy and relax, leaving you to do all the heavy lifting in a relationship. It can be pretty exhausting too for a woman because in the natural order of things, you should be the chased and not the chaser. It may not bother you at first, but keep at it for the long haul, and soon you will not be able to stop wondering whether he loves you at all or not.

Let him call you; don't call him. If you want to hold him even more in your metaphoric grip, then observe the three-call rule. The rule is simple; do not call a man often. Instead, call him once for every three calls. Try it! Even if you have been calling him forever, it is time to wean yourself off that phone and learn to stop calling him as though your life depended on it. Keep your hands away from the phone; frankly if you are sitting at home staring at the phone and waiting for him to call, then you desperately need to get a life. Go read Chapter Ten again. It is okay if he calls and you are out to, say the movies with a girlfriend. It will actually do you both a world of good if he spends all evening wondering where you are and what you are doing and with whom. Just knowing he could lose you to someone else should keep him on his toes.

The true power to dictate whether a man treats you right or walks all over you during the course or your relationship rests with you; use it well!

3. Make him think of you often by leaving little notes in his briefcase

Men have this almost Neanderthal urge to brand a woman as theirs especially because of some ancient, instinctive need to warn off other rivals. So when he grabs your hand at a bar, or introduces you loudly as his girl, he is not doing that because you look hot enough to catch fire; he is doing that to let other men know you are taken— yes, men do have their fair share of jealousy.

So once you have a man's attention and he starts proclaiming you as his, he is in effect branding you as his. Well in that case, it's time to do a little branding of your own— on his mind.

See the weird thing about men is that more often than not, if you constantly attempt to overtly show how much you love them, they will end up pushing you away or running as far as their legs can carry them.

Subtlety is key.

Brand yourself onto his mind by putting little notes in his briefcase for him to find. If your relationship is already sexual, then you can just let your inner naughty side come out to play. Write sexy, little notes filled with innuendos and promises that hint at what you are going to do to him as soon as you clap eyes on him. Trust me, he will be home so fast, it will make you dizzy.

But if your relationship has not strayed into the sex arena, just leave little notes reminding how much you care for him and how attractive he is; it will leave him with a warm, special glow. And yes, he will hurry over to see you.

4.   Remain as hot as ever

Okay so I am guessing when he met you, you were probably waxed, plucked, and groomed well enough to rival Cleopatra. Now this is where most of us are guilty; we let ourselves go down the line. We forget that there are worse things than being ill-prepared for opportunities that come our way. Every relationship is an opportunity to touch someone's life profoundly but I do wonder how you are going do that if you start to repulse them before you have even had a chance to do any touching. Don't get me wrong, you could change from a size 6 to 16 in the space of a month and a man would still love you, but if you start looking unkempt and worn down in the bargain, he may start looking elsewhere. In this scenario would you really blame him?

I have met men who dig women of different shapes and sizes, but I am yet to meet a man who digs a dirty, unkempt woman; unless of course he is too unkempt himself to notice— a scary thought.

Listen not everybody has to be a size double zero, but if you are overweight, you can do several things about it from workout, to steam baths to dieting.

Sometimes, men tend to feel tricked when they start out with a diva and end up with a bedraggled, nagging fishwife with her hair standing in every direction. I mean everybody has a bad day now and then but if you really do stop grooming yourself, eating right, and dressing right, he *will* start to lose interest— and fast!

5. It's okay to worry about him

Remember how you felt all warm, loved, and wanted when he worried about your sore throat and also that time he drove all the way downtown for some aspirin and ice just because you stubbed your toe? Well when he does have the flu, you have full permission to worry about him *and* show it.

Men love it when women worry about them because of course it shows caring and more often than not, it stems from a place of love. Feel free to bring him a warm bowl of chicken soup and cluck sympathetically while you shove it down his sore throat; but even then, don't baby him. Men have fragile egos hiding beneath their brawn and muscles but they will deny it with their dying breath and any hint treating him like a child may not go over so well.

You really don't want to overdo the worry bit because you are bound to start treating him like a little boy without realizing it. See the problem is, if he is like most men, he probably adores his Mum, he just doesn't want to date her. Worrying constantly about him makes him feel emasculated; yeah I gaped too when I heard that one. In truth though, it makes him feel as though you are doubting his capability to be a man and take care of himself; he starts feeling like he has to prove himself to you just like he does with his mum. It wears thin after a while though and he would most likely lose interest in you and your ability to make him feel like a pupil with his hand in the cookie jar.

CHAPTER FOURTEEN

Small Things to You Can Be a Big Deal to Him

Keeping a man's attention fixed on yourself for the long haul is a somewhat tricky thing especially when there are so many attractive, super-hot, available women flitting around in his orbit but if you read all the way to this point, you should be just fine.

There are some other things you might want to keep in mind though:

1.   Don't bother trying to change him

Let me put it this way; hell would freeze over and leopards would change their spots before men would change who they really are. More often than not, people end up in relationships with jerks because they think they would change down the line; they usually don't unless they experience something closely resembling an epiphany.

The real tragedy would be dating a perfectly great guy and attempting to change him just because he is not 100% perfect. Don't try to change him, he is a human being not a mannequin; no one is perfect. If he's too much of a jerk for you, get out of that relationship as fast as you can. If his flaws are manageable, learn to tolerate. Trying to change a man is like mothering him and nothing makes him lose interest faster.

Besides, whatever you think of as flaws, someone else may actually find endearing and actually love it. For instance, his five-foot three height that embarrasses you every time you have to introduce him to a friend who is six-foot plus, is actually what someone else somewhere wants in her dream man. If he is not good enough for you, don't toy with him; don't try to change him; just pass him over so he can find someone else who thinks of him as her McDreamy.

2.   Play with him

Being able to just let the child in them come out is an uphill battle for some people. In truth though, you should learn to just let that inner child come out every now and then because then, it means you are in touch with every part of yourself. No matter how stuffy and serious a guy may seem, he would love it if you played with him every now and then. Couples who learn to play silly and laugh together often have better chances of surviving the ups and downs of relationships than couples who do not.

Besides running around and jumping like kids establishes a bond like little else. Shared laughter creates great memories that forge an even stronger bond between the both of you which is a good thing because true relationships are about weathering the storms of life together.

Every now and then, do something totally out of character like start a pillow fight with him or a tickling match. These are some of my favourites and I have found that surprisingly, tickling matches with all the attendant laughter and body contact are as powerful a turn on for him as good ol' foreplay. Go figure!

3. Do not possess the persona of a needy woman

Yes men love rescuing you, and blah blah but if you morph into this clingy, needy insecure person that calls him every minute and dogs his footsteps everywhere, he will start finding ways to avoid you. Worse, even when he does allow himself to be in your company, he will feel trapped, bored, and even resentful; you don't want that! Trust me, you really don't! Nothing erodes self-confidence faster than feeling your significant other does not really want you.

It's great to ask his help every now and then because he is the very person who should swoop in and rescue you when he can. But learn not to ask for unnecessary stuff and avoid making him feel he is being taken for granted. No one likes that and you will definitely not like his reaction; I'm guessing it would be kinda like the way Chicken Little was ignored after he cried false one time too many.

4.   Don't try to tell him what to do

Again, unless he is Mama's boy, he will not like this nor will he appreciate it. And hey, even if he *is* Mama's boy, he won't thank you for pointing out the obvious with your actions and rubbing it in his face.

Sometimes men like to talk to the women in their lives; tell them their problems. Do not imagine that just because he does this that you have all the answers or that he expects you to jump in and fix it like a modern-day Indiana Jones.

Men are natural fixers; once they have a problem, you can bet your sweet ass they are already thinking up solutions. But if he tells you expressly that he wants or needs your advice, then you can proffer a solution. But take care never to be that girl who leaps from listening to trying to fix it in a nanosecond particularly when he has not asked you to do that.

5.   Don't let him place you on a pedestal

Unless you are pure white, on four legs, with a long straight horn sticking out of the very top of your head, you are not perfect. And heck, even the unicorn isn't very perfect either; I mean just because it is the stuff of fairy tales does not mean it is completely harmless does it? Those horns do look sharp after all.

A man who really likes you may understandably fall into the error of thinking you can do no wrong and placing you on a pedestal. Well in truth, you would not be human if you pretended not to enjoy being in that position. In reality though, it is a very delicate and precarious place to be because inevitably, you will screw up and make a couple of truly horrible mistakes that will shove you off the pedestal and send you crashing back to earth with the rest of the masses. It won't matter then how little the mistake is, how much he is overreacting or how good you were in the past. What would matter is that you broke his expectations and disappointed him. When that happens, the thud you hear will also be the sound of your relationship breaking all over the place.

Let him know you have your fair share of faults, but do not harp on them too much or over-magnify them so that they do not become the only thing he sees. A man will overlook a number of personal flaws — as well he should since we all know how perfect he is — but when he has to discover them on his own like some big, dirty secret, he may feel deceived and put off.

So do not exaggerate your failings, but don't hide them and pretend to be a Saint either.

6.   Surprise him — in a good way

Most people will tell you upfront that they hate surprises; well that's okay because most people are liars. People generally love surprises especially the good kind of surprises. Men are natural daredevils and are adventurous so every now and then, feel free to plan a cruise or a skydiving experience or heck, just good old skating but don't tell him about it; just surprise him.

Surprises that involve pumping adrenaline through his system are a very good idea because it then means you get to make him feel good about himself and about you without resorting to sex.

If he thinks you are an adventurous, fun-loving girl, you may be certain he will be reluctant to leave you.

7.   Make his life easier

In a world filled with stress, most people are unable to fully relax and unwind until they come home. Let him have peace and quiet at home rather than haranguing him with a barrel of worrisome questions the moment he steps over the threshold.

Every now and then, encourage him to take time out for himself. A man needs to unwind just as much as you do you know and the fact that you can once in a while suggest that he stays in with popcorn and his favourite game on television will tell him more than words that you are thinking of him and watching out for his welfare.

8.   Wear his favourite colour every now and then

Yes the girl in your favourite rom-com had the right idea; wearing a man's favourite colour every now and then is a good call because it shows you listen to him and you know his likes or dislikes. It also tells him unmistakeably that you value his opinion and you want to please him.

Sometimes, it could be that he particularly loves you in a particular dress. In that case, wearing it for a special night out with him tells him that you want to look good for him no matter how long you have been together. Red is particularly an aphrodisiac to men but if his favourite dress is another colour, wear it once in a while and he will not only admire you, it will register in his subconscious that you are thoughtful and mindful of what he thinks.

9.   Do not be afraid to call him out

While you are all sugar and spice, you don't have to pretend to be someone you are not. Never sacrifice your personal principles for anyone; yes despite how amazing his baby blues may seem. If you like a man and he does something you do not like, feel free to call him out on it. No, this is not your cue to demand satisfaction at dawn with pistols drawn; this simply means you should not let him get away with treating you badly. Don't harangue him needlessly, just let him know he hurt you. If his behaviour was really bad, I am all for ignoring his calls for the next three days at least. Yes he may think you are high maintenance if you do, but which would you really prefer: to be treated like crap because you are so accommodating and tolerant or to be treated with some modicum of respect and finesse because he is afraid you will throw a hissy fit if he does not? Exactly. Besides of which, men actually love high maintenance women, no matter how much else they may protest otherwise.

But a word to the wise, while you may rant and rave and cuss out his behaviour, be careful so you don't cross the line and bruise his ego; he may never forgive that one.

10. Respect him

I saved this one for last because it is so important I wanted it to stick. A man can live without many things like your love (shocking but true), your trust (cue the unrepentant cheats) and even your family's approval of him (I think that is kinda of obvious) but the one thing he cannot live without is your respect. Men crave respect kinda the way women crave love. A man may forgive you many things but disrespecting him is going be a hard sell especially if you do it in front of witnesses.

Men are frightfully protective of, and aware of their image which is why if you do not respect them, you have threatened something at the very core of their self-esteem. A man needs his self-confidence in spades and if you threaten that, he will find it easier to break things off with you.

Marriages and long term relationships have hit the rocks permanently because he man felt he was not getting the respect he deserved. If a man is attracted to you, I assure you that you could very easily demolish that attraction in two seconds flat by disrespecting him. He will often go away and stay away. The same is true for a long term relationship. In fact, write this down so you don't forget it; a man needs your respect every single minute of every single day. If you find yourself in a relationship with a man you cannot respect, get out fast because you can't win with this one.

There are a lot of things which seem little at first blush but which can affect, in the long term, his interest in you. If you want to keep a man's attention, you need to understand that several things can make his attention stray and more often than not, it is up to you to look out for those things and try to manage them as much as possible.

CHAPTER FIFTEEN

Your Grandmother Was Right

Yeah, just when you thought you had escaped this one, here it is. The way to a man's heart is through his stomach; and you can yawn as loudly as you want to, it's still true.

No one — meaning me — has said you have to turn into a Stepford wife just to keep a man latched onto you. If you are busy (and let's face it, in today's world who isn't?) your career could suffer terribly if you decide to take on preparing his breakfast, lunch, and dinner; unless of course you are a gourmet chef and your office is a five-star restaurant that delivers takeouts.

Men are generally receptive of good food and when you have someone who is not so good at cooking, it is a great way to show you care because of course it means you put effort into it. The best part is, if you can prepare his favourite food without asking him, you win a lot of bonus points with him and make him feel very special.

When you cook for a man, you can help monitor his diet and actually help him keep in shape. You don't really want to start nagging him about how his pot belly is beginning to rival that of your seven months' pregnant neighbour; that will just get him pissed off and cause him to withdraw. If you want him to be on the same page as you, simply start switching up his diet. Instead of fat, cheesy food, give him healthier but tasty meals. In time, his gut should start to reduce to a level approaching your idea of perfection. You are happier, and he is none the wiser. Hey, even if he is, it won't matter to him because you were able to handle it without nagging or making him feel like a fat, giant, beached whale.

When you prepare a gourmet feast, it really is your call how it is served up. This means you can turn your effort into a romantic dinner for two and thus spend more time with him without seeming obvious. In fact, since you slaved so hard for dinner, feel free to put on something sexy and wow him. Do not forget to light a few candles and get Barbra Streisand on the sound system.

Cooking for a man is a definite route to plant yourself firmly in his heart but you do not want to do this too often if you are not in a committed relationship. If you constantly cook for a man you are not in a committed relationship with, it will just come off as trying too hard and he may end up taking you for granted.

There are a few more interesting facts about cooking for a man, especially if you are in a committed relationship. First off, since you basically control what he eats, you can totally feed him aphrodisiacs like oysters, honey, dark chocolate and even figs. I hear the lowly banana is a wonderful 'turn on drug' too; which means you could always whip up a fruit salad for him interlaced with lots and lots of banana and serve it up with a straight face.

Sex in the kitchen is taboo and insanely hot; if you need to put the spice back into your love life especially if you have been a couple for years, then look no further. After you have wowed his stomach, you may be sure he will start feeling frisky especially if you are looking especially hot while the bananas and honey are going to work in his body.

Oh and if sex in the kitchen is also on the menu, make certain you remember to have a shower and spruce up a little after cooking, before eating. I mean consider how all your hard work will go down the drain if he tries to feel you up after dinner or breakfast, only to find you smelling like onions.

CHAPTER SIXTEEN

Make Him Crave You

No matter how possessive you think women are, women have got nothing on men in that department. When it comes to being possessive, men are even worse than women.

Men are sadly prone to getting seriously lazy down the relationship lane especially if they feel all is good. Often, they just want to kick back, relax and act like the whole world is at their feet; and in that case, it is up to you to shake things up. If it were up to a man, he could go an entire year without telling you he loves you because in his book, you already know that.

If a man really likes you, nothing zaps him out of his idle comfort faster than the fear of losing you to some other sharp dude. Men are not lazy by nature but they often tend to wear themselves out throwing things around, going to work, or just hanging with their buddies. If they do this often enough, they start to ignore you more and you start to feel neglected.

This is the part where you need to make him jealous, but without being obvious because if he suspects what you are doing, he may retaliate or worse, act even more unimpressed which would just tear your nerves to shreds:

1. Buy sexy lingerie

No don't buy him a tie; that will just make him feel more confident. Buy yourself some sexy lingerie and make sure they are lying around where he is bound to see them. Don't make this too obvious; just dump your shopping bags on the bed with a hint of the lace peeping out. Don't wear it for weeks though and he will wonder why you bought such sexy lingerie if you are not going to wear it any time soon. Can't you just *see* the scary images that will be flitting through his brain at this point?

2. Join a unisex gym

Mention in passing the names of several male friends you make at the gym. Feel free to rhapsodize about their bulging biceps and how good they look. If you want to be extra naughty, chatter 'innocently' about how some of your male friends from the office have taken to coming to your gym too. He is a guy so he will be pretty sure he knows what they are thinking; and no, he won't like it at all.

Don't feel offended if he stonily suggests that you change your gym or just pretends to be deaf and dumb even while grinding his jaw hard.

Just try to hide your laughter when he puts his feet down and insists that you change into something less tight when next you are going to the gym. In fact, he may cause your jaw to drop to the very ground by joining you to the gym.

3.   Use your friends

Get your girlfriends to send you Valentine's Day roses without cards and watch his face turn an interesting shade of red. He will be furious especially if you don't even bother trying to ask if the roses are from him. Look happy and put your flowers in water. You may rest assured he will not forget roses next Valentine's Day or your birthday; whichever comes first.

Also, you could go on serious fun outings with your friends and make sure that they are in on what you want to achieve. Have raving fun and take pictures to document them. Seeing pictures of how great your life is even in his absence, on Facebook, instagram and other social media are bound to make him have the urge to suppress a twinge or two of jealousy.

It's good for you and it's good for your relationship; it means you have a life of your own. He is part of your life and not your whole life.

4.   Attract the attention of other men

This is basically a no-brainer. Make sure you are dressed to kill the next time you go out together and if any man smiles at you, smile back. No don't flirt in front of your guy because frankly that would be a tad disrespectful but don't ignore appreciative glances form other guys either. Make certain to work with what you have by wearing sexy, low cut dresses; grooming your appearance and even making certain that you have on killer heels that accentuate your legs and make them appear to go on for miles. Dress sexy enough to dazzle and make sure you laugh a lot that night and have a good time. If his eyes don't catch fire from watching other guys watch you, then you really have to admire his restraint.

Arrange your hair in a long, flowing, sexy do and make certain to toss it every now and then. There is just something about watching a woman's attractive mane that makes men go crazy. A man is infinitely attracted to a woman's hair for several reasons and watching other man watch you play with your hair will make him see red.

Don't be afraid to step out onto the dance floor with other men either if he does not want to dance; just be careful not to cross the line from tickling his jealous bone to appearing cheat. Other than that, flirt with everyone but him.

5.   Accept other dates

Okay this may be a little tricky if you are married, but if you are in a long term relationship where you feel neglected, feel free to accept dates from other men. If you show him that other guys are interested in you, his natural competitiveness will kick in. He will start competing with them to win your affection and frankly, he sees it as a signal that you are putting him on a timer. He will be likely to come through now.

Now if you are just in a relationship and looking for s definite commitment from him, make certain to turn him into your confidante. Every now and then, ask his views on the various guys chasing you and ask which one he thinks may be best.

Trust me, no matter how he answers, he will be choking back bile and you may just force his hand.

Jealousy is perfect when it is coming from the guy as far as I am concerned. It just makes him cherish you more.

But jealousy is really a double-edged sword so be careful how you wield it. If you are going to attempt to make him jealous, I would suggest you question your motives first and make sure you are not doing it for the wrong reasons.

If you want to make him jealous in a bid to get him to stop being so neglectful of you, then there is absolutely nothing wrong with that. In fact, it is the way to go.

Some women also try to make a man jealous as a way of giving him a taste of his own medicine say, because he flirted with someone else. In this scenario, if this does not work it usually could indicate that you have been wasting your time with someone who is just stringing you along. Sometimes, the mirror effect is a powerful tool; let him witness firsthand the effects of his flirting.

CHAPTER SEVENTEEN

Understand Him

Liking a man and understanding him are two entirely different things. If you are involved with a man but have a hard time understanding him, you can't really blame him if he is somewhat reserved around you, now can you.

Contrary to public opinion, men also value trust highly in a relationship and if you do not understand him even after spending a few months or years together, he will naturally be unable to fully trust you.

Besides, knowing your significant other understands you often makes people react by falling even more in love with him or her. Remember that time you were so upset because your best friend stealthily bought the exact same shirt as yours and he understood why you were so upset without you having to explain? We both know it leaves a very warm feeling in the pit of your stomach when you realize your significant other knows you even better than you know yourself.

When it comes to men, being able to understand them pushes you even further on his priority meter because men are not as expressive as women; they are trained from birth to hide or control their emotions. So the fact that you still somehow got under all of that to see what he really feels of thinks about something underneath will make him believe that you really care for him. It will also tell him that you are observant and he will want to spend even more time with you because you have just paid him a backhanded compliment. It is a compliment to him because it's like you are saying that he is special enough that you took your time to study and get to know him better.

Now every man is different mind, but there are some basic rules that remain true of all men in relationships which you really should get for both your sakes:

1.   He will not be as blunt with you as he would a friend

Yes he loves you more than he ever imagines he could ever love anyone, but because of that there are some things that he may be uncomfortable telling you. No, this is not the time to pull on your nagging slippers and attempt to ferret his secrets out of him. Understand him. Men may be unable to tell you some things because they do not want to hurt you, they do not want to disappoint or repulse you; or they are scared your reaction would hurt *them*. Yes this last simply stems from a healthy instinct for self-preservation but the others are simply a direct result of his desire to preserve what you have going.

Either way, secrets do not help either of you and most times, the problem with secrets is not the content but how they are discovered. For instance, imagine he feels the need to hide say the fact that he has a child by another woman from you, it may hurt you to learn that, but not as much as it would hurt if you found out on your own.

Talk to him and use your reactions to let him know it is okay to confide in you.

2.   He does not do too well with emotions

So you want to do a near scientific dissection of Gone with the Wind and he is all grumpy, bored, and actually cuts you off mid-sentence; don't feel bad. It's nothing personal. Guys have a hard time talking about emotions. It does not mean he loves you any less nor does it mean he does not enjoy seeing you happy or hearing how much you love him; it's just how men are. You can't really change it. I mean if a man were to sit around talking about his feelings all day, he's probably gay; and even with gay men, not all of them can handle the feelings thingy.

3.   He loves games

Whether it's juggling three girls at once in their daily lives or smashing villains and freeing damsels left and right on play station III, men love games. There just seems to be something about games that speaks to his adventurous side and makes him feel better about himself.

A man can zone out in front of the television set in dirty boxers, playing games, thinking ahead on how to win and whatever. It's a fantasy world where he can be a hero.

Once in a while in real life, let him feel like a hero too. Give him manly chores like asking him to repair the kitchen cabinet or some such thing. If he claims to be too busy (which is highly unlikely) then invite the hot neighbour over and ask him to repair the cabinet. I guarantee that when he walks in and sees this man sweating in your kitchen, all bulging muscles while you stand quietly by like the little woman with hero worship in your eyes, he would never again refuse to help out. If he does help out, praise him as casually as possible; it will mean a lot then. You could just say something like, "You are so strong to be able to do that on your own." He would puff out his chest and may even attempt to leap your kitchen table in a single bound just to prove how strong he is.

4.   He is not as hygienic as you would like

Some men are neat-nicks true, but more often than not, men are unable to truly comprehend why you throw a hissy fit every time they leave the toilet seat down or leave their dirty socks lying around or wear the same boxers twice in a row. One friend broke up with her boyfriend after she caught him wearing the same boxers after sex. It is truly gross and disgusting but men are not usually the neatest people on the planet.

You could try telling him about the toilet seat *ad nauseum*, or you could just find an alternative; like try putting your head through a wall. Some men will catch on eventually but even if he does not, try not to get too angry because he really isn't doing it on purpose.

5.   His eyes will always search out pretty women.

No matter how much he loves you, he is not blind; and even if he is, he may still notice pretty women. Men admire pretty women but the mere fact that you do does not mean that they would go ahead and cheat. Some men do yes, but you should try to understand your guy to know what category he belongs.

Women do admire handsome men too, but less often than men and studies have shown that women who are in happy relationships are less likely to admire other men. Unfortunately the same is not true for men.

But if he starts letting his eyes feast on other women right in front of you, I do believe you are right to worry and you can go ahead and let him know that this bothers you.

6.   It is not always a good time

Yes this is the part where I remind you that men are usually terrible multi-taskers. If he has just come home from work, he probably wants a cold shower (or a warm one depending on your climate) and the last thing he needs to hear just as he is coming in the door is how you gave his landlady the finger for daring to suggest that her rose garden looked better than yours. Be wise in dealing with him. Let him unwind, rest, get some good food in his stomach and even feel you up a little before you start dissing your landlady to him.

Understanding your partner is a great tool for success in keeping his attention because it makes him feel appreciated and important. It is also wonderful for you too because the better you understand him, the harder it would be for him to get away with lying to you and the result is that you would trust him more.

Understanding a man is tricky business because different men have different sides really. You have to keep the channels of communication wide open but never start with that 'We need to talk' business women love to use so much. That will just put him on the defensive and get him ready to lie on oath or withdraw from the conversation.

CONCLUSION

As with most other things in life, reading a book about how to catch and keep his attention will not do much in the way of helping you catch and keep his attention unless of course you are able to practice the things in this book. Catching a man's attention is a piece of cake if you know what you are doing so get on out there and make him sit up and take notice.

In the end though, it's true that nothing is ever worth it if you are not happy. Forcing yourself into a relationship you don't want, just for the heck of it or just because all your friends are paired up, is a bad idea. And if you are already in one and he is causing you stress or sadness, end it; you will be better off, and so will he.

BONUS FOR THE LADIES

A must watch - The Single Most Important Thing To A Man .
. .

It takes a lot to shock me, but this video made me go "Wow."

===>> **http://tinyurl.com/l8usq4y**

It's by this guy named James Bauer and it explains the single most important thing to a man when it comes to having a relationship.

===>> **http://tinyurl.com/l8usq4y**

If you think guys are "complicated" or "hard to figure out" you really need to watch this video now.

Fighting for Your Passion,

Rachel Rose

P.S. After he reveals the "most important thing," James shows you how to trigger this one critical emotion in your guy to draw him closer to you and make him almost addicted to you long term.

What I really love about what James says is that it's not manipulative or "game playing."

===>> http://tinyurl.com/l8usq4y

BONUS FOR THE GUYS

(Ladies you will LOVE this too)

Below is my #1 Recommended Program
for my ALL Male Clients.

I have never recommended any other program over this one.

Listen to me guys…

3 Things You Can Do To A Woman To Give Her The Best Orgasms Of Her Life

Do your wife a favor and go to this link.

http://tinyurl.com/k6k6xjf

Conclusion

Thank you again for downloading this book!

If you enjoyed this book, then I'd like to ask you for a favor, would you be kind enough to leave a review for this book on Amazon? It'd be greatly appreciated!

Help us better serve you by sending questions or comments to rachelrosebooks@gmail.com - Thank you!

Printed in Great Britain
by Amazon